MW01093696

Philosophy

Polity's *Why It Matters* series

In these short and lively books, world-leading
thinkers make the case for the importance
of their subjects and aim to inspire a new
generation of students.

Helen Beebee
Michael Rush

Philosophy

Why It Matters

polity

First published in 2019 by Polity Press

Polity Press
65 Bridge Street
Cambridge CB2 1UR, UK

Polity Press
101 Station Landing
Suite 300
Medford, MA 02155, USA

ISBN-13: 978-1-5095-3215-5
ISBN-13: 978-1-5095-3216-2 (pb)

A catalogue record for this book is available from the British Library.

Library of Congress Cataloging-in-Publication Data

Names: Beebee, Helen, author. | Rush, Michael, 1976- author.
Title: Philosophy : why it matters / Helen Beebee, Michael Rush.
Description: Cambridge ; Medford, MA : Polity Press, 2019. | Includes
   bibliographical references and index.
Identifiers: LCCN 2018032465 (print) | LCCN 2018051371 (ebook) | ISBN
   9781509532186 (Epub) | ISBN 9781509532155 | ISBN 9781509532155
   (hardback) | ISBN 9781509532162(paperback)
Subjects: LCSH: Philosophy.
Classification: LCC B72 (ebook) | LCC B72 .B44 2019 (print) | DDC 100--dc23
LC record available at https://lccn.loc.gov/2018032465

Typeset in 11 on 15 Sabon by Servis Filmsetting Ltd, Stockport, Cheshire
Printed and bound in Great Britain by CPI Group (UK) Ltd, Croydon

For further information on Polity, visit our website: politybooks.com

Contents

Acknowledgements

We would like to thank Pascal Porcheron and Ellen MacDonald-Kramer at Polity for their encouragement, enthusiasm, efficiency and good advice, as well as three anonymous reviewers, whose comments and suggestions led to many improvements.

Thanks to Al Baker for conversations on a book idea that led to a different book idea that led to a different book idea and ended up here. Thanks also to the following people for reading and commenting on a draft of this book: Sammy Boardman, Matthew Elton, Harry Gray, Jasmine Hay, Anneli Jefferson, Pauline Kwiat-Hodson, Emilia Meissner, Matthew Rush, and Ema Sullivan-Bissett. You're all great.

We dedicate this book to the memory of Harry Lesser (1943–2015): an inspiring teacher, generous colleague, and friend.

Introduction

Perhaps you are reading this book because you're interested in knowing more about how philosophy might be relevant to your life and your understanding of the world around you. Perhaps you are reading this book to help you decide whether to study philosophy more formally; maybe you are wondering which courses to take at university. We firmly believe in the value and interest of philosophy at every stage of every walk of life. Philosophy matters.

Philosophy matters because it seeks and promotes understanding and clear thought and because it is practically helpful, intrinsically interesting, and culturally and historically significant. Those are grand claims, but in this book we'll show you why we think they're true. Philosophy is not the only valuable discipline, of course, and each has its role in the

1

collaborative effort to understand the world, but philosophy has an important and distinctive part to play, as we will see.

As well as being important, philosophy is also misunderstood: it might not be what you think it is. The good news is that philosophy is all around you and there's a strong chance you've asked yourself distinctively philosophical questions already even if you didn't know that's what you were doing. If you've ever asked yourself whether parents should be allowed to demand risky and expensive medical procedures for their children; had a passionate argument about whether Rachmaninoff is *really* better than Rage Against The Machine; puzzled over how we can tell whether our elected leaders are lying to us for their own gain and whether we should be concerned if they are; wondered whether you can believe that physics tells us how the world really is and also believe in God; speculated about whether we have free will and some measure of control over our actions or are at the mercy of unconscious natural processes – just like when you slip on the ice or the leaves fall from the trees – then you've taken your first steps in philosophy. All of these are philosophical questions and all of them are questions that might occur to you as you make your way about the world.

Introduction

We can engage with these questions to some extent without any deep knowledge of philosophy. Most people do just that, but it is also possible to engage with them more fruitfully, more fully, and more satisfyingly once you know a bit about the philosophical theories and methods that define the questions and constrain the sorts of answers we can reasonably give. Philosophy allows you to be interested in all the things that already fascinate you but to engage with them more deeply. This is why philosophy matters to you. Once we all engage more deeply with the sorts of questions that face us we can live more richly and we can start to expose the sort of sloppy thinking that works against the smooth running of the world and is used by some people to maintain positions of power and influence over others. This is why philosophy matters to everyone.

There are a variety of fair reasons why you might have got hold of the wrong end of the stick about what philosophy is. Perhaps philosophy wasn't taught at your school; it isn't very widely taught in schools. It is just well enough known in the public imagination for it to have been lampooned, without being well enough understood for the jokes always to be recognized as jokes. It concerns itself with abstract questions that don't always lend themselves to casual conversation.

As a result, you might think that philosophy is just a matter of expressing your opinion, or that it involves sitting around all day wondering whether your chair exists. You might think that philosophy is really just like theology or some other religious pursuit, or that it mostly involves meditation. You might even confuse philosophy with psychology. Historically that's not ridiculous, since psychology started out as a branch of philosophy, though they parted ways more than a century ago now. Or you might think that philosophy is something that was only done a long time in the past or that, though it's still done today, it is only indulged in by people in dusty libraries where they can't do any harm or get in the way.

There is a common usage of the word 'philosophy' that people have in mind when they say things like '"Seize the day", that's my philosophy!' or they ask, 'So what's your philosophy, then?' We can make sense of those uses of the word, but that's not what philosophers mean by it. Philosophers also don't mean the same by 'philosophical' as you might if you reported that someone was being very philosophical about receiving some bad news.

What philosophers do mean by 'philosophy' – and we know this isn't going to be very helpful right now – is just that collection of principles, theories, techniques, methods, and questions that we're hoping to give you a sense of in the rest of this book. It's a collection that is bound by some common themes of rational inquiry, critical reflection, and systematic thought, but its subject matter, as we'll see, is splendidly varied.

What's important to remember is that there is no kind of person with a monopoly on philosophical potential. Look in the mirror: if that's not already a philosopher you're looking at, it's a potential philosopher. Whether you're considering taking up the formal study of philosophy, you're already studying philosophy, or you're just interested to see why these wouldn't be ridiculous things to do, this book is for you.

You might expect a book about philosophy to be chock-full of names of philosophers and lists of their achievements, but we've trimmed that right down here because what is important is seeing how you can take the methods and techniques of philosophy and apply them to things that you care about or are interested in. It's not about people, it's about ideas.

It would be wrong to suggest that only those who study philosophy in a rigorous and managed way are capable of indulging in philosophical thoughts, or that the benefits of philosophy are open only to those people. As we've said, the beginnings of philosophy are already all around you. What *is* true is that there is a body of knowledge and a collection of systematic methods that it's possible to learn; it's possible to be better or worse at the skills of philosophical reflection and analysis. This isn't a textbook outlining the body of philosophical knowledge, or the history of philosophy from its beginnings in the ancient world, and it isn't a book about one particular great philosophical tradition among those that developed in Greece, India, or China.

At its root, philosophy is about the systematic understanding of our ideas and the logical assessment of our arguments. It encourages serious reflection, rigorous thought, and the clear expression of sometimes complex and difficult ideas. If we want our lives to be intelligible, if we want to discuss and debate coherently with other people about questions across the wide range of issues we've already mentioned and more, we need to be able to be confident that the terms and concepts we employ in these conversations are themselves coherent and that we don't accidentally contradict ourselves or talk past each other. Some of these terms have a clear impact on very important social questions. If we do not try to clarify what the terms 'right' and 'wrong' mean, we cannot understand what is going on in a debate

Introduction

about whether a proposed invasion of another country is right or wrong, or whether it is right or wrong to provide a publicly funded service allowing people to choose to die by euthanasia. If we do not critically assess what makes something a work of art, we cannot fully judge, compare, or appreciate some of the most important contributions made to civilization by some of our finest minds.

Or to take another example: we usually assume that we have free will. Perhaps you've never explicitly thought about that, but it's an assumption in the background whenever we deliberate over important decisions, or spend time planning what to have for dinner. We think we can make genuine choices, and we tend to assume that this involves being able, prior to choosing, to go either way. It turns out that reconciling this belief with other philosophical and scientific ideas that seem plausible is surprisingly difficult.

Doing justice to our intuitive beliefs about the world whilst at the same time doing justice to our scientific understanding; deciding how to modify our political inclinations in the light of our ethical commitments; understanding the difference between belief and knowledge to help us decide which ideas to commit ourselves to: all these, and more, are philosophical questions.

Introduction

As we've said, the importance of these activities is not confined to the formal study of philosophy, but one of the things a formal study of philosophy can give you is an expertise in and a familiarity with a set of techniques, strategies, and intellectual tools that can be developed and honed and which can positively inform discussion and debate in many different arenas.

The chapters in this book take a series of general themes – aspects of our lives or the world around us that we might want to try to understand more fully – and explain how philosophy can contribute to our understanding. We're going to introduce you to some philosophical theories as we go along. It's worth saying now, and worth remembering as you read this book, that all these theories are seriously and thoroughly disputed and no consensus has been reached. Far from being something to worry about, this is a consequence of avoiding dogma and remaining open to revising our theories as new evidence and insights emerge. This is a strength that philosophy shares with the sciences when each is done well. You may well have come across some of these theories before, but they may not have been presented as things about which you could have sensible doubts, and the level of current and ongoing debate will almost certainly have been downplayed. You will also have learned, especially in science lessons at school, the well-established theories, and it's understandable that in these cases you lose sight of the fact that once there were loads of live options. Philosophy is even more like that than many areas of the sciences: there are lots of current philosophical possibilities on which we need to reflect. Assessing these competing theories and explanations is one excellent way in which you can hone your philosophical and analytical skills. Indeed, getting better at the skills central to philosophy essentially involves actively doing philosophy and not just passively learning about what other philosophers have said. You need to get engaged for yourself!

The rest of this book aims to give you a glimpse of some of the possibilities and some of the tools, strategies, and techniques that will help you get engaged in philosophical debates in just this sort of way. In chapter 1 we consider how we can better understand ourselves: what sort of thing am I? What does it take to be a human being? Might I continue to exist after I am dead? Do I have free will? Chapter 2 looks at understanding public debate. How do we tell whether our politicians are telling us the truth? Does it matter whether they do? We also consider the more general question of wanting our beliefs as far as possible to be true. Chapter 3 is about under-standing the world. Can science tell us everything we need to know? Are there distinctively religious truths? Can we believe in God and maintain a com-mitment to the success of physics? What counts as evidence in favour of scientific or religious views? Chapter 4 asks how we ought to behave towards each other. How should we be allowed to treat people? What rights do we have that we are entitled to expect other people to respect? The conclusion rounds things off with a quick tour of some of the things that philosophers think about that wouldn't fit in the book (there are loads!) and suggests some ways of answering the broad questions with which we started this introduction.

We hope that these themes are ones that resonate with you. We've all encountered some religious practices, witnessed and maybe taken part in public debates, judged someone to have behaved well or badly, formed at least some simple scientific beliefs, and wondered what happens after we die. Philosophy matters because most of us are, to some degree, philosophically inclined, even if some of you didn't realize it until right now.

1

Understanding Ourselves

What am I? What is it to be human? Could I continue to exist even after I'm dead – so that, in principle at least, I might go to Heaven or be reincarnated as a donkey? What's the relationship between my mind and my brain – or are they just the same thing? If there are differences between men's and women's brains, does that mean that differences between men's and women's behaviour are innate and therefore inevitable? Do I have free will, or am I merely programmed to behave in certain ways by my brain and my environment?

These are all excellent questions, and they are, broadly speaking, *philosophical* questions – or, at least, the kind of satisfying answer you're looking for might not be one that the sciences can answer, or at least not on their own. Take the first two on the list. Ask a biologist what the answer to the first question is, and they will probably give you a funny look. *What are you?* You are a human being, a member of the species *Homo sapiens*. Job done. Next question: *what is it to be human?* Easy! It's just to be a member of the species *Homo sapiens*.

Did that answer your questions? Probably not. You probably knew all of that already, so if you were asking the questions in the first place, those probably weren't the kinds of answer you wanted. So: try asking a philosopher instead and see what happens. Better still, ask a philosopher to give you some basic equipment – some concepts, some suggestions about how you might approach the questions, some arguments for you to evaluate – and then try to figure out the answers for yourself.

Humans, Persons, Brains, and Minds

Let's start again in a more philosophical vein. Our biologist was right, of course: we are, all of us, human beings – that is, members of the species *Homo sapiens*. In some sense, that *is* what we are. (Philosophers are very fond of saying 'in some sense'. Normally what it signals is that the claim being made can be read in various ways, and that it's important to distinguish between them.) But does being a human being *define* us? Is it what is *essential* to us? We might try to start answering that question by asking what it is that's *special* about us human beings. There are, of course, various features that human beings have that nothing else has (so far as we know). But there's nothing that special, in and of itself, about having opposable thumbs or having two legs and two arms. And some features that you might think are special about us aren't even the sole preserve of human beings, such as the ability to communicate or to think. Plenty of other species can communicate with each other – by barking or chirping or doing a waggle dance or whatever. Similarly, it looks as though some other species – dogs, for example – are capable of at least rudimentary thoughts: Rover wants a treat, and he believes that if he does his trick for you he'll get one.

Perhaps, then, the feature of human beings that *is* special – the one that really matters to us – is our capacity to have certain *kinds* of thought. For example, we are not just conscious of the world around us but *self*-conscious: we can think about ourselves. You can not only daydream about cake; you can also reflect on the fact that you've just spent ten valuable minutes doing that, and wonder whether your time might be more productively spent. We can make long-term plans, and we can think of our lives as having a kind of narrative structure to them. We are also able to think in distinctively *moral* ways. And so on. Let's call a being that has those sorts of mental capacity – and admittedly we haven't defined this very precisely – a *person*.

We should note that this is a controversial proposal: philosophers disagree about what it is to be a person. As you will find repeatedly in this book, philosophers disagree about pretty much everything; and you'll probably find that we make plenty of claims that *you* disagree with. But that's just the way things are: uncertainty is something you have to learn to love if you want to do philosophy. The important thing is that you don't just think, 'Oh, *that* answer's wrong', but you stop and consider *why* it's wrong, what a different answer might look like, and why that answer might be better. Philosophy isn't just a matter of thinking critically; it also involves being creative. If you think a particular philosophical view delivers the wrong answer to a question you care about, or it doesn't solve a problem it was supposed to solve, your job as a philosopher is to think of a better view – one that gives the right answer or solves the problem.

According to the way of thinking about ourselves just described, *being a person* need not in principle be a feature that only, or indeed all, members of the species *Homo sapiens* have. An alien could easily be a person. Most aliens depicted in science fiction *are* depicted as persons, in fact. A really, really sophisticated android could be a person: think of Officer K in *Blade Runner 2049*, or Data in *Star Trek*. Maybe in very many thousands of years – if they survive that long – other great apes might evolve into persons. Perhaps in principle a person doesn't even need a physical body at all. If God exists, perhaps God is a person.

With the notion of *personhood* in place, it looks as though when people ask the second question on the list we began with – what is it to be human? – they don't really want a biological answer ('It's just to be a member of the species *Homo sapiens*'), and hence probably aren't really asking the question they wanted an answer to. Really, what they want to know is: what is it to be a *person*? We've given a very rudimentary and provisional answer to that question. But it's a start.

And it leads us back to the first question: *what am I?* Well, you know you're a human being. You also know that you're a person. We might think of our question as a question about which of those is more important. Which captures your essence: is it your physical or biological status as this particular living and breathing flesh-and-blood creature? Is that what makes you what you are? Or is it rather your status as this particular person: the being that has a particular narrative history involving your past experiences and (we hope) future experiences that accord with your long-term goals, the being that has particular important relationships with other people, a particular set of core values, and a sense of their place in the world? Needless to say, philosophers disagree on which of these options is correct.

How you answer this question makes a difference to how you then go on to ask other questions. Take the next one on the list: *could I continue to exist even after I'm dead?* Well, suppose you think it's of your essence that you're this particular flesh-and-blood human being. Then the answer is easy: it's 'no'. A corpse is still made of flesh and blood until it's cremated or decomposes sufficiently, but it's not a living-and-breathing creature – when you die, *you* will cease to exist. On the other hand, if you think it's of your essence that you're this par-ticular *person*, then it looks as though, in principle at least, the answer could be 'yes'. The residents of Heaven (and indeed Hell and Purgatory), if such there be, are, presumably, still persons. Or maybe you could in principle continue to exist after your death in other ways: perhaps, one day far in the future, scientists will be able to upload all of your psychological traits onto a hard drive and then, when you die, defrost a body they cloned earlier and download them into that, so that you have survived but in a new body.

Think about what happens when you upgrade your phone. The new phone might be better in various ways – a crack-free screen, enhanced functionality, more memory – but you can transfer all the stuff that's important to you: your apps, your address book, your diary, your photos, and so on. It's a different phone, but they're the same address book, diary, and so on. If what's important to being the same *person* is a matter of keeping the analogue of the photos, apps, and so on, rather than the analogue of the physical phone that houses those things, then the future-scientist scenario above really would mean that *you* have survived.

The idea of 'uploading' someone's psychological traits from one body and then 'downloading' them into a different body brings us to the next question on our list: *what's the relationship between my mind and my brain – or are they just the same thing?* Since we've already mentioned the possibility of continuing to exist after your death, let's start there. Let's assume that being *you* really is a matter of your psychology rather than your flesh-and-blood body. As we said before, that opens up the possibility, in principle, that you could survive your own death – as most of the world's major religions say you can. But *in what form* might you survive your own death? It's one thing to say that in principle you could continue to exist – or to be the same person – in the absence of a physical body, but surely all of those psychological traits have to be traits of *something*.

Well, let's think about Heaven. According to the standard story, when you go to Heaven (or the afterlife), you leave your earthly body behind. So what is it that 'goes' to Heaven? Well, Heaven isn't a place. You can't plot its co-ordinates on a map of the universe; you don't turn left at Alpha Centauri to get there. It isn't a physical thing, and it correspondingly doesn't have a location. Similarly, according to (say) orthodox Hinduism, Islam, Christianity, and Judaism, the thing that goes to Heaven or ascends to the afterlife or gets reincarnated isn't physical either: it's the *soul*. The soul is the thing in which all of our psychological traits are to be found, and it's what, along with those traits, continues to exist after we die. (The story according to Buddhism is much more complicated and – we think – philosophically a lot more interesting. A core doctrine of Buddhism is that there is no such thing as a 'soul' or 'self'. Rather what we misleadingly refer to as the 'self' is really an ever-changing flux of mental characteristics that are somehow bundled together without 'inhering' in any distinctively non-physical substance.)

Let's get back to our question: *what's the relationship between my mind and my brain – or are they just the same thing?* Probably anybody who believes in the soul should say that the mind and the *soul* are the same thing. After all, the soul is supposed to be the thing that does all the mental stuff – thinking, experiencing, deciding, imagining, and so on. So such people should think that the mind and the brain *aren't* the same thing, since the soul most definitely is not the brain – the brain is a physical thing and the soul is not. That's logic for you. If A is the same thing as B and B is not the same thing as C, then A is not the same thing as C.

But what if you don't believe in the soul? And, in particular, what if you think that really all there is to a person – or any other actual being, for that matter – is physical stuff, whether it's flesh and blood and bones or metal and silicon and electrical circuits? Then what? Is the mind just the brain or not? And if not, what on earth *is* it?

We think that the question is a bit misleading. Really the right thing to say is that 'the mind' isn't really a *thing* at all. Instead, *having* a mind – although it sounds like it amounts to possessing a thing, just like having a bicycle – is really a matter of having various psychological capacities (exactly *which* capacities being a question we'll leave open). And those psychological capacities are 'implemented in' or, as we'll say, 'realized in' the brain.

The notion of 'realization' needs some explaining. Again, thinking about phones might be helpful. If you're old-fashioned and have an actual physical diary made of paper, and you buy a new bag, you might transfer the diary from your old bag to your new one. The diary is a physical object that you can shift from one place to another just by picking it up and moving it. But transferring your electronic diary from your old phone to your new phone isn't like that at all. There is no *bit of stuff* that is extracted from the old phone and put in the new one: if you opened up your phone, you wouldn't find a little lump of stuff that is your diary, another lump that is your address book, and so on. What's happened instead is that a lot of information was recorded by your computer when you backed up your old phone – encoded somehow in its circuitry – and thence encoded in the circuitry of your new phone. The diary is 'realized' in the circuitry of the phone, and what's crucial to its being the *same* diary after you've switched phones is that it still does all of the things you needed your diary to do: it still has your deadlines and events there, just as you wanted it to have. It doesn't matter at all that the phone itself is a different phone; nor, indeed, does it matter *how* the diary is realized in the circuitry.

Similarly for the mind and the brain, we think: the same mind could be 'realized' in a different brain, just as your (electronic) diary can be realized in a different phone. And it's not just the mind as a whole. We have not just a mind, but also beliefs, desires, memories, plans, aspirations, character traits, and so on. We talk about these things as though they are, well, *things*. You can list ten of your beliefs just as easily as you can list ten of the things on the table in front of you. But – as with the diary on your phone – you can't, even in principle, peer inside someone's brain and find a little nugget labelled 'the belief that Seoul is the capital of South Korea' or 'the intention to go shopping on Wednesday'. Instead, 'things' like beliefs and desires and intentions are 'realized' in your brain in a way that is (in some sense!) a bit like the way that a particular diary entry ('Dentist at ten o'clock') is realized in the circuitry of your phone.

So that's the first three questions on our list ticked off. Well not really, of course. What we've really done is give you some tools for thinking about those questions: some distinctions you might not have thought of before, some (we hope) helpful analogies and examples, some useful terminology, some arguments that you might want to criticize or improve on, and so on. We hope that you thought from the outset that the questions are questions that matter: how can it *not* matter what we are, or whether we can survive the death of our bodies? And so we hope to have gone at least some way towards convincing you that philosophy matters – since, at least when it comes to these particular questions, philosophy is the right tool for the job.

On Men's and Women's Brains

Let's move on to the next question on our list, which is a particular favourite of ours: *if there are differences between men's and women's brains, does that mean that differences between men's and women's behaviour are innate and therefore inevitable?* It's a particular favourite because the thinking that lies behind the question is one that you hear routinely when some clever neuroscientist discovers some difference between (most or many) men's brains and (most or many) women's brains. And the argument often goes something like this: '*See?* Neuroscience shows us that men and women are just *different*. It's just hardwired. That's why, for example, nurses tend to be women and consultants tend to be men, or women tend to be better at multi-tasking and men tend to be better at single-minded attention.'

We said in the introduction that one reason why philosophy matters is that it can help to expose sloppy thinking. You might think that appealing to some recent bit of scientific evidence is, by definition, the opposite of sloppy thinking. That, unfortunately, would be a mistake: it all depends on how you're arguing from your evidence to your conclusion. So let's debunk the argument just described, shall we?

Let's start by assuming that your psychology – all of it: your beliefs, your character traits, your preferences, the full works – is 'realized' or encoded somehow in your brain. Roughly speaking, the view we're assuming here is known as 'physicalism': the view that absolutely everything is somehow made of or 'realized in' physical stuff. Of course, you might not buy that assumption. In particular, if you believe in God or the soul you won't buy it, since neither of those things – if they exist – is made of physical stuff. But if you reject the assumption, here's an exercise for you: figure out whether the argument we're about to give works out if you don't assume physicalism – and if not, why not?

If physicalism is true, then if two people differ psychologically in some way, their brains are going to differ in some way as well. For example, suppose Mo can speak fluent Urdu and Amir can't. Then – given physicalism – there must be some physical difference between them. And, since people's language abilities are going to be encoded in their brains and not in, say, their toes, that physical difference is going to be a difference between their brains: Mo's brain must be different in some way to Amir's brain. The same goes if Jane can work out 32 × 32 in her head and Jack can't, or if Shaun can remember how 'Bohemian Rhapsody' starts and Shayane can't. And so on.

Maybe at some point in the distant future neuroscientists will be able to scan or probe people's brains and tell on that basis which languages they're fluent in, or how good they are at mental arithmetic, or which tunes they can remember. Or maybe not; it doesn't matter. What matters is that psychological differences between people entail that there *are* differences between their brains, whether or not anyone can, or will in the future be able to, locate those brain differences.

So here are two questions. Grant that there must

indeed be such differences between Mo's and Amir's, and Jane's and Jack's, and Shaun's and Shayane's brains. What exactly can we infer about whether or not those differences are innate – differences they're born with? And – relatedly – what can we infer about whether or not the differences are things that none of these people can do anything about? The answer to both questions is: precisely nothing. Nothing at all. Mo was not born with the ability to speak fluent Urdu. Nor was Jane born with the ability to multiply numbers together in her head, or Shaun born somehow knowing how 'Bohemian Rhapsody' starts. Moreover, we have no reason at all to think that Amir, Jack, or Shayane cannot change their brains in such a way that they then *will* be able to do those things. And they don't need to do any dangerous do-it-yourself brain surgery to do that; they just need to immerse themselves in an Urdu-speaking environment for a while or do a lot of work on mental arithmetic or make an effort to remember the start of 'Bohemian Rhapsody'. Change features of your mind and you – quite literally – change features of your brain too. That's just physicalism for you.

That's not to say that there are *no* brain differences that different people are born with that do or might make a difference to their mental capacities or character traits or whatever; nor is it to say that we can change just *any* feature of our brains. If Amir were a cat rather than an eight-year-old boy from Toronto, his brain would definitely lack whatever features brains require in order for the owners of those brains to learn to speak fluent Urdu. We don't need neuroscience to tell us that, of course – we already knew that about cats. Doubtless some people's brains, at the time of birth, make them more or less capable than others of learning a new language or doing mental arithmetic or memorizing tunes. But we absolutely can't infer that there *were* such differences at birth just from the fact that there are, now, differences in the brains of people who were born quite a while ago – people such as Mo and Amir, for example. Nor can we infer that, now or in the future, Amir is incapable of learning to speak Urdu.

So, back to our original question: *if there are differences between men's and women's brains, does that mean that differences between men's and women's behaviour are innate and therefore inevitable?* Well, we've just argued that the differences between Mo's brain and Amir's brain, as they currently are at the age of eight, don't imply that those differences are innate or inevitable. For all we know, at birth Amir's brain was constituted in such a way as to make it entirely possible for him to have learned Urdu given the right environment or training. Equally, for all we know, Amir is, now or in the future, entirely capable of learning Urdu. And there is just no reason at all to deny that what goes for Mo and Amir – or indeed speakers and non-speakers of Urdu in general – goes for men and women.

So the answer to our original question, we hope to have convinced you, is a resounding 'no'. Women may, for example, be better – in general – at, say, empathy than men. Let's just assume that that's so. In that case, there must be some corresponding difference in the parts of their brains that are responsible for empathy. Does that tell us that there must be *innate* differences between men and women? No it doesn't – just as the fact that Mo can speak Urdu and Amir can't doesn't tell us that there must be innate differences between *them*. Does it tell us that any particular woman can't become less empathetic, or that any particular man can't become more empathetic? Again, no – just as the current differences between Mo's brain and Amir's brain don't imply that Amir can't learn to speak Urdu. Job done.

It's important to be clear on what we *haven't* established here. We haven't established that there are no innate or inevitable differences between men's and women's psychological characteristics.

All we've established is that you shouldn't infer that there *are* such differences from the existing neuro-scientific evidence. But it's worth pointing out that there are plenty of facts available that *do* seem to do a pretty good job of explaining why there are some general psychological differences between men and women – facts that have nothing to do with neuroscience. Just think about the very many differences between the ways that boys and girls are brought up: which toys they're given to play with, how much emphasis is placed on how pretty they are, what kinds of expectations they absorb from their parents and teachers and the culture they're living in about how they should behave, and so on. These facts come to us not from philosophy or from neuroscience but from other disciplines – sociology, social and developmental psychology, and so on – though of course there is a lot of scope for philo-sophical input on these issues. When it comes to answering the questions that matter it's a collabora-tion, not a competition.

Free Will and Neuroscience

And so to our last question – and it's the big one: *do I have free will, or am I merely programmed to behave in certain ways by my brain and my environment?* Well, let's start with an old experiment from the 1980s by the neuroscientist Benjamin Libet. Your head is wired up via some electrodes to a machine that measures electrical activity in your brain. The experimenter asks you to flex your wrist whenever you feel the urge to do so over a period of a few minutes. You're looking at a clock with a fast-moving hand, and, whenever you *do* feel the urge, you're asked to report where the hand was when you started to feel it. Whenever you flex your wrist, the machine records the electrical activity that was going on in your brain just before you did it.

What the experimenters found was that typically there was a big spike in electrical activity around 350 milliseconds (about a third of a second) *before* the experimental subjects reported they had first felt the urge to flex their wrists. In other (possibly misleading, as we'll see) words, their brains 'knew' that they were going to feel the urge to flex their wrists before the subjects were consciously aware of that urge.

A lot of people, including a lot of neuroscientists, have concluded from this and similar experiments that there is no such thing as free will. Here's a sample headline, from *Scientific American* (28 April 2016): 'What neuroscience says about free will:

We're convinced that it exists, but it may just be a trick the brain plays on itself'. It's easy to see how one might jump to this conclusion. After all, it looks as though your brain had already 'decided' that you would flex your wrist before you had even felt the urge to do so. So *you* weren't really in control of what you did – your brain was.

There are a lot of things to say about what would be wrong with jumping to that conclusion, however. Here are some of them. First, your brain didn't *decide* anything. Brains don't make decisions, or for that matter feel a bit under the weather or fancy a nice slice of coffee-and-walnut cake – *people* do. Those decisions are 'realized' or 'implemented' by their brains (we're assuming physicalism again here). So whatever your brain was doing, it wasn't making a decision.

Second, it's a pretty huge leap to go from 'you weren't exercising free will when you flexed your wrist' to 'nobody exercises free will, ever'. Even if we agree with the first claim, we need not accept the second. Perhaps – once you've agreed to go along with the experiment and hence to simply flex your wrist whenever you feel like it – you really aren't exercising free will. We care about free will because we care about having control over our own destinies and taking responsibility for our actions.

Just doing things when you feel the urge to do them *is*, in a way, a failure to exercise free will. It doesn't follow that we *never* exercise free will. When you're deciding what to study at university or confronting a moral dilemma, you're precisely *not* merely following your urges: you're weighing up different considerations and trying to figure out what the best course of action is. We, the authors, would eat enormous quantities of cake if we merely followed our urges. Our actual cake consumption, however, is quite modest because we are (often) able to override those urges and do what we think it best to do instead.

OK, but what if the neuroscientists could somehow devise an experiment where you were asked to make a *decision* – say, the decision to eat that slice of cake – and they got the same result, namely there was a spike in brain activity just before you decided? Let's imagine that we have such a result on the table. Even if we grant that your brain did not *decide* to eat the cake, isn't there still something alarming about the idea that your decision was somehow pre-programmed or determined by what was going on in your brain? Isn't it obvious that a decision that is pre-programmed or determined in this way is one that is not made freely?

We probably don't need to point this out, but

philosophical opinion on this matter has been divided for centuries, and the debate shows no sign of being resolved any time soon. Some philosophers think that acting or deciding freely does indeed require that your action or decision was not determined by what went on (in your brain, your upbringing, your environment, or wherever) before. And they think this because they think acting freely requires the *ability to do otherwise*, and they think that ability requires lack of determination by those past factors. So they think that you only *freely* decided to pass up the kind offer of cake if you could have accepted it instead, and they think what *that* requires is that all of those past features of you and your environment – including what went on in your brain just beforehand – left it open whether you would accept or decline the cake.

Others disagree. Some of those others agree that acting freely requires the ability to do otherwise, but they deny that that ability requires lack of determination by past factors. They will point out, for example, that abilities are in general things that we retain even when we are not exercising them, and indeed even when we are determined not to exercise them. For example, you are probably able to do some of the things on this list: ride a bike, play the piano, tie your shoelaces. Those aren't abilities that you only have when you are doing those things; they aren't even abilities you only have when you are in the vicinity of a bike, a piano, or your shoes. Similarly for the ability to decide to eat the cake you've just been offered: that's an ability you had at the point where you decided not to; it's just one that you did not (and perhaps were determined not to) exercise.

Still others deny that the ability to do otherwise is required for acting freely in the first place. Often they make the case for this claim by appealing to the idea that moral responsibility – being praiseworthy or blameworthy for one's actions – requires acting freely. Suppose your kindly and public-spirited nature – a character trait you have worked hard to maintain and develop throughout your life – genuinely determines that, when you see the pedestrian in front of you drop their wallet, you walk over, pick it up, and give it back to them. By assumption, it was determined by your circumstances and your character that you would do that. But if acting freely is required for moral responsibility and acting freely requires the ability to do otherwise, then you are not praiseworthy for returning the wallet to its owner: because of your kindly and public-spirited nature you could not have done otherwise, so you didn't act freely, and so you were not morally responsible for what you did. That just sounds plain wrong to some philosophers.

Why does the debate about free will matter? One reason why it matters is the connection we just mentioned between free will and moral responsibility. Things like praising and blaming people, resenting what they do if they deliberately upset you and deciding whether or not to accept their subsequent apology, and being grateful when they are kind to you, play a really important role in our relationships with other people. But if there was no free will, then moral responsibility would be a myth: nobody would ever deserve praise or blame, or gratitude or resentment, and they would never have any reason to apologize for anything. Maybe our lives just wouldn't make sense to us if we gave up on the idea of holding people accountable for their actions. On the other hand, some philosophers think believing in free will is bad for us: it legitimizes the thought that people truly deserve blame and punishment and thus encourages vindictiveness, guilt, and shame – all things we would be better off without. Which side is right about that? We're going to leave it to you to think about that question.

2

Understanding Public Debate

At the time of writing, one of the biggest topics of international news is – and has been for quite some time – Donald Trump. Trump is, of course, a highly political topic; but for the purposes of this chapter, we aren't going to focus on the politics. Rather, we're going to focus on issues surrounding the very nature and underpinnings of public and political debate – issues that Trump raises in a particularly vivid and disturbing way.

A 'debate' in the traditional sense – the kind that happens in debating societies or in government assemblies and senates such as the UK's House of Commons or the US's House of Representatives – is a situation where people with opposing beliefs – about the wisdom of some proposed piece of legislation, or about abortion or euthanasia or capitalism or whatever – set forward their reasons for believing what they believe, and try to come up with reasons *not* to believe what their opponents believe. 'Debate' has come to have a much wider meaning; a 'public debate' about something is often merely a matter of people expressing their views in public or semi-public forums: in the newspapers, on social media, and so on. The inexorable increase in the use of the internet has simultaneously made public debate much easier – anyone with internet access can very easily find out about pretty much any topic, and engage in an exchange of views on it with friends and strangers alike – but also much more unruly.

The internet is, of course, an extraordinary tool for finding information, but it is also, unfortunately, an extraordinary tool for finding *mis*information. And it can be very hard to tell the difference: which news outlets and Twitter feeds should we trust and which should we steer clear of? How do we distinguish between the reputable sources and the troll factories, or between the news stories that have been rigorously researched and those based on a handful of rogue tweets from people who are the internet equivalent of arsonists, lobbing their incendiary claims out into the Twittersphere just to provoke a response?

Those are hard questions to answer. But there is

a more basic and distinctively philosophical question lurking here, which is: does it *matter* whether we can sift the information from the misinformation? That's the first issue we'll be addressing in this chapter. The second issue – for which the first sets the stage – relates more directly to Donald Trump, and concerns the *trust* that we place in other people as sources of information – especially political leaders. Why is trust important in the context of public debate? In order to answer that question, we'll need to consider what trust is, and how exactly it is undermined by politicians who – for example – blithely assert falsehoods on social media and dismiss every news story they don't like as 'fake news'.

Before we start, though, a word about the role that philosophy is playing in this chapter. Chapter 1 was pretty overtly philosophical. Much of this chapter isn't; indeed, much of it might simply strike you as just plain common sense. And so you might wonder: where has all the philosophy gone? The answer is: sometimes philosophy *is* just a matter of, well, common sense. Or – as it's sometimes put – 'refined common sense'. Sometimes what philosophers do is not set themselves some very abstract question and set about answering it armed only with a blank piece of paper and a pencil; sometimes they start from the everyday ways in which we go about our lives and try to figure out what is going on and why, in a distinctively philosophical – but not necessarily abstruse or highly theoretical – way.

That's largely what's going to happen in this chapter. We'll be asking – for example – why it's good to have beliefs, why it's good to have true rather than false beliefs, what kinds of thing count as evidence for a belief, and how testimony works. Those are all questions that arise within the area of philosophy known as *epistemology*. The fact that you might be able to go at least some way towards answering them yourself, without having studied epistemology before or knowing any technical terms, doesn't make the questions any less philosophical.

There are plenty of much more abstruse questions one can ask in epistemology – trust us on that! But we'll be staying away from them because the issues we'll be focusing on in this chapter – live, practical, and important issues that affect all of us – don't really require too much by way of abstract and technical theorizing.

Evidence and Belief

Let's start – naturally – with the first issue identified earlier: does it matter whether we can sift the information from the misinformation? Well, as you go about your daily life, you constantly rely on your beliefs. We don't mean this to sound deep – we're not talking about the belief in God, or in the fundamental goodness of humanity, or whatever (although you may rely on beliefs of that kind too). Rather, we're talking about completely mundane beliefs. If you really, really want a banana and lack any beliefs at all about where to find one, you're going to be stuck. If you want to be in Tokyo by 11 o'clock, you'd better have a range of beliefs – or acquire those that you currently lack – about when the trains leave, how long they take to get to Tokyo, how long it will take you to get from home to the station, and so on.

In general, it also really helps if our beliefs are *true* – otherwise we'll often find ourselves thwarted in our attempts to achieve what we want to achieve. If your belief that the shop is open is false, your attempt to buy a banana is going to result in a wasted trip and no banana. If your belief that the Tokyo train leaves at 8.15 is false – perhaps because you have misread the timetable – then you may fail to make it to Tokyo by 11 o'clock.

It depends on the details, of course. If the train in fact leaves at 8.18, you're probably still going to be OK; in this case, all your false belief costs you is the minor inconvenience of having to wait an extra three minutes on the platform and arriving three minutes later than expected. But in general, having true beliefs is a good thing because you base your actions and plans on your beliefs, and if those beliefs aren't true, things are quite likely not to work out the way you wanted them to.

This applies, of course, not just to our everyday business of eating bananas and catching trains, but to our engagement in the social and political spheres as well. If you have a vote in an upcoming referendum about, ooh, let's say, whether or not to leave the European Union, and what you care most about is, say, the state of the National Health Service, then – if you're rational – you'll vote according to whether you believe staying in or leaving the EU is more likely to improve the NHS. But, again, it matters whether that belief is true. If (say) you vote 'leave' because you believe that leaving the EU will mean that the government will spend £350 million extra per week on the NHS – as was repeatedly and very prominently claimed by the actual 'leave' campaign in 2016 – then it matters a lot whether leaving the EU will in fact have that result. If it won't, then in casting your 'leave' vote you will have failed to help bring about the outcome you wanted to achieve.

A quick aside on truth. The nature of truth is a very thorny issue amongst philosophers. However, one thing they pretty much all agree on is that a sentence 'p' is true if and only if p. 'Today is Tuesday' is true if and only if today is Tuesday; 'Seoul is the capital of South Korea' is true if and only if Seoul is the capital of South Korea, and so on. This being so, you should be just as confident that, say, the sentence 'Seoul is the capital of South Korea' is *true* as you are that Seoul is the capital of South Korea. This is important because people sometimes seem to think that believing that a given sentence 'p' is *true* is somehow much more demanding than just believing that p. It isn't. If you confidently believe that God exists, or that Serena Williams will win the US Open next year, then you should also believe – equally confidently – that it's *true* that God exists (equivalently: the sentence 'God exists' is true), or that it's true that Serena will win the US Open next year.

Having *true* beliefs is important to us, then: generally speaking, it helps us get what we want. So how do we go about getting true beliefs? And in particular, how do we sort the true from the false? The very short answer is: by acquiring *evidence*. We'll have more to say about the nature and variety of evidence in the next chapter, where we discuss science and religion. For now, just listing some common-or-garden sources of evidence will suffice.

Perhaps the most basic source of evidence is that provided by your senses. You can check whether you bolted the back door or whether there are any bananas in the cupboard by going and taking a look. You can find out whether the heating is on by touching the radiator. And so on. (Here's one of those questions in epistemology that we're ignoring: how, if at all, can we be sure that we aren't being massively deceived by our senses all the time? That's the problem of scepticism.)

A very large number of our beliefs are not, however, based on direct experience of whatever it is we have a belief about. Beliefs about the future are one kind of case: unfortunately there is no way to directly check whether the bus is going to arrive on time unless you have a time machine at your disposal. You're going to have to rely on *past* direct experience – the bus has generally arrived on time in the past – and *infer* that it's going to arrive on time today. (Here's another question we're ignoring: what, if anything, justifies drawing conclusions about the future based on what's happened in the past? That's the problem of induction.)

Often, though – whether the belief in question is one concerning the future or not – we rely on *in*direct sources of evidence. Never having caught a train from New York to Boston before, you have no direct past experience to rely on when it comes to forming a belief about when the next train leaves; you have to consult an online timetable, or the departure board at Penn Station, or whatever. Your evidence for your belief that if you dial this number you will get through to your friend's phone is that that's the number listed in your address book. Your evidence that the oven has now reached the desired temperature is that the light just went off. (That's your own experience, of course, but it's not *direct* experience of the temperature of the oven. You're relying on the assumption that both the thermostat and the light are working properly.) And so on.

None of these sources of evidence – not even the direct evidence of our senses – is *completely* reliable, of course. That glance at the door doesn't *guarantee* the truth of your belief that it's locked; maybe you didn't quite put the bolt all the way up, so it looks locked even though it isn't. Maybe you made a mistake typing that number into your phone's address book, or maybe your friend has changed her number since you last spoke. Maybe – just maybe – what looks like a delicious banana is really made of plastic, and someone has planted it in the cupboard in order to deceive you. Nonetheless, in general, if we are careful (and setting aside the problems of scepticism and induction just mentioned), we are pretty good at using the evidence available to us in a way that tends to deliver true rather than false beliefs, at least when it comes to eating bananas, catching trains, and arranging to meet our friends. And we're pretty good at adjusting our evidence-gathering procedures when they start letting us down: once you've realized that that phone number isn't working, you'll stop using it and try to find out what the right number is.

Telling the Truth

One really important source of evidence – and the one that we're going to focus on in the rest of this chapter – is other people. Any time you believe something because you read it in a newspaper or a history book or on Facebook, or because someone told you in person, you're relying on another person, or perhaps other people, as a source of evidence. Evidence of this kind is known as *testimony*. Very roughly, we can think of testimony as 'second-hand' evidence. When you ask someone the way to the station and they tell you it's straight ahead and then left at the bank, you're expecting them to have evidence for that claim. You don't know what this evidence is – maybe they just came from the station themselves, or maybe they live here, or maybe they just happen to have looked at a map a couple of minutes ago and noticed where the station is, or whatever – but you *trust* that in volunteering this information, when they could simply have said 'I'm sorry, I don't know', they really do have good evidence for what they say. Similarly, if you read a popular history book it will make lots of claims about the past but will probably tell you nothing about what the author's evidence is for making those claims. Again, in coming to believe what the book says, you are trusting that they really do have evidence, even though – again – you have no idea what that evidence is.

Is testimony a reliable source of evidence? Well, we all know – even if we haven't explicitly thought about it in the abstract before – that the answer to this question is: 'it depends'. For example, we all have some friends who are prone to exaggeration or who will report things as unassailable known facts when they just read them in a tabloid newspaper gossip column, and we have other friends whom we think of as very reliable sources of evidence on any topic at all because they tend not to say things without good evidence.

Relying on testimony is a tricky business for a number of reasons. One is that, as we've just seen, when we rely on someone's testimony we generally don't know what that evidence is, or even whether they have any. When the stranger tells you that the station is straight ahead and then left at the bank, you're just going to have to decide whether to trust them or not; asking them to explain to you what their evidence is would not be a polite thing to do. Another reason it's tricky is that, even when someone does cite their evidence, you are not in a position to evaluate that evidence for yourself. Often a newspaper report *will* tell you something about the evidence the journalist has for making at least some of the claims they make; they will have photographic evidence, cite sources (thus themselves relying on testimony), statistical data, or whatever. But of course whether the evidence they cite is itself reliable is something you aren't really in a position to judge. Are the unnamed 'sources' or 'friends' themselves reliable sources of information? Has the photographic evidence been doctored? Have the statistical data been manipulated or misinterpreted? In this kind of case, we generally have to resort to very general beliefs (for which we may in turn lack very good evidence) about the journalistic stand-ards that the newspaper generally upholds: do they have a track record of manipulating photographs, for example? How often do they publish retractions and apologies concerning previously reported celebrity gossip?

Another problematic thing about testimony is, of course, that people sometimes simply *lie*. It's not just that they lack sufficiently good evidence for saying what they are saying; they are actively and deliberately trying to get you to believe something that they themselves know or believe to be false. How on earth can we tell whether someone is simply lying to us when we are not in a position to have a conversation with them about whether they really believe the claim they're making? There's no easy answer to that question.

So we've seen so far that (a) true beliefs are good things to have, (b) relying on reliable sources of evidence for your beliefs is a good way of making it more likely that your beliefs are true, and (c) in the case of testimony in particular, it can be extremely difficult, and sometimes pretty much impossible, to work out whether the person whose testimony you are relying on is making the claims they make on the basis of a reliable source of evidence.

Earlier, we said that the answer to the question 'Is testimony a reliable source of evidence?' is: it depends. That's true, of course – it *does* depend.

But let's abstract away from particular cases for a moment and ask whether there are any reasons for thinking that testimony *in general* is a reliable source of evidence. Are we entitled to assume, as a kind of default position, that by and large people reliably tell us the truth? We think the answer to that question is 'yes' – but, as we'll see later on, we're worried about significant threats to that position.

The claim that testimony is indeed generally (but of course by no means always) a reliable source of evidence is one that we'll argue for in a somewhat roundabout way, starting with the claim that telling the truth is a *moral norm*. (This is a controversial move, but, as we've said before, pretty much all moves in philosophy are controversial.) Testimony, as we've said, comes from other people. And people – unlike thermostats or laptops or smartphones – are subject to moral norms: rules or codes of conduct that we (mostly) know we should abide by as we go about our daily lives. We know that we should not steal or deliberately harm other people or leave the dog in the car on a hot day with the window closed. We suggest that one such moral norm is that we tell the truth. More precisely, we should only say things for which we have good evidence – that is, things that we have *good reasons* to think are true. If you go around saying things for which you lack good evidence – or indeed things that you have good reasons to think are false – you violate that moral norm.

There are obvious exceptions. Nobody expects an author to be telling the truth in a novel: the fact that Mr Darcy never really existed does not reflect badly on Jane Austen. Similarly, when a stand-up comedian tells you a funny story about what happened to her the other day, you don't *really* expect her to be telling the truth. It doesn't really matter to us whether it's true or not; it only matters that it's funny. There are other kinds of exception too: when the armed burglar asks you where the jewellery is and you figure that telling him, falsely, that it's in the next room will buy you just enough time to escape from the house and call the police, it's OK to go ahead and lie. Working out exactly when it's OK not to tell the truth is a difficult business: when your friend asks you whether you like his new haircut, should you tell him it looks great even though you think it's terrible? Is it OK to tell small children that Father Christmas exists? But the fact that it sometimes *is* OK to lie, or to say things you don't have good evidence for, does not undermine the claim that we should *in general* tell the truth. (Occasionally it's probably OK to steal – say if stealing is for some reason the only way you can save someone's life. That doesn't undermine the fact that *in general* we shouldn't steal.)

Suppose, then, that telling the truth is indeed a moral norm. Now, do people – by and large, of course, and certainly not without exception – tend to abide by moral norms? We think the answer to *that* question is 'yes'; and we think there is ample evidence for that answer. Just consider how many people you come across as you go about your daily business, and think about how rarely, in the grand scheme of things, people violate moral norms. How often – out of all the countless times that any of these things *could* happen every day – are you deliberately tripped up or sworn at by a random stranger, or mugged or burgled, or overcharged in a café? Very rarely (unless you are exceptionally unlucky). That being so, you're entitled to assume, at least as a default position, that most of the time, most people don't violate moral norms. And so, if telling the truth is a moral norm, you're also entitled to assume – again as a default position – that people will tell you the truth.

Or, at least, you are as things currently stand. But we think that entitlement is under threat.

Bullshit

By and large, we've said, people *do* tell the truth – but unfortunately not all of us do that all of the time. One way to fail to tell the truth is of course to lie – to deliberately say something false. But even liars tend to at least implicitly *acknowledge* or be sensitive to what we'll called the 'norm of truth'. Imagine Shaun wants Shayane to miss her train and so he tells her that the station is over to the right, when he knows full well that in fact it's over to the left. Shaun is lying, but he is still acknowledging the norm of truth, even though he is violating it. It matters to him whether what he says is true or false because he wants Shayane to come away with a false belief and not a true one so that she misses her train.

But now imagine that when Shayane asks Shaun where the station is, he just says the first thing that comes into his head. He really doesn't care whether it's true or not. Perhaps he just wants Shayane to go away as quickly as possible, and giving her some directions – any directions – will do the trick. He doesn't care at all whether she goes away with a true belief or a false one, so long as she goes away. In that case, Shaun isn't really *lying*. For one thing, he might be telling the truth; perhaps the first thing that comes into his head is in fact the right way to get to the station. But if so, that's just an accident – he didn't say what he said *because* he thought it was the truth. And if he is *not* telling the truth, again he isn't really *lying* because he isn't trying to *deceive* Shayane; as we've said, he doesn't care whether she ends up with a true belief or a false one. Shaun is simply not acknowledging or being sensitive to the norm of truth at all.

Shaun is definitely behaving badly in this second example, since he has failed to make any effort to tell the truth. But what exactly *is* he doing, given that he's not lying? Fortunately, thanks to the philosopher Harry Frankfurt, there is now a technical term for what he's doing, and that term is *bullshit*. To bullshit is to say something without caring whether or not it's true.

Someone might bullshit for any of various reasons. Internet trolls are probably mostly bullshitters; mostly, we assume, they do it because they simply want to have an effect – they are, as we put it earlier, the internet equivalent of arsonists. Not only do they not care whether what they say is true, they don't really even care what they're saying at all, so long as it gets a lot of people steamed up enough to post angry responses. People who parrot the views of their boss or of someone they are trying to impress as though those views are their own, without considering whether or not they themselves really believe those things, are also bullshitters. They may have good practical reasons for bullshitting – perhaps the only way to avoid the sack is just to agree with everything your boss says – but they're still bullshitting.

Donald Trump indulges in a lot of bullshit. Unlike your average internet troll, he *does* care what he's saying; he wants people to believe that he is a brilliant president, that he is doing a great job, that he is clever and popular. But (we submit) when he tries to make people believe these things through tweets and speeches, he often does so with no concern at all for whether or not what he says is true. Like Shaun, he isn't *lying*; he just doesn't *care* about the norm of truth.

Consider some examples: 'The American public is fed up with the disrespect the NFL is paying to our Country, our Flag and our National Anthem' (tweet, 28 May 2017). Well, is it? Have there been any (methodologically sound) surveys conducted amongst the American public on whether they thought the NFL players who knelt during the National Anthem were disrespecting anything, and, if so, whether they were fed up with it? We think not. Or: 'The best taco bowls are made in Trump

Tower Grill. I love Hispanics!' (tweet, 5 May 2016). Really? How many taco bowls has Trump consumed elsewhere, exactly? And has he really considered whether he *really* loves Hispanics? (If he had considered that question, he might have asked himself whether it might be a tiny bit racist to make a judgement about an entire minority ethnic group on the basis of the deliciousness of tacos.) Or take the demonstrably false claim, made on Twitter on 18 June 2018, that 'Crime in Germany is way up.' In fact the 2017 figures showed that the crime rate in Germany was 9 per cent down on 2016, and 4 per cent down on 2012.

What is distinctive about these kinds of comments is the fact that Trump simply seems to be completely *unconcerned* about whether or not they are true; truth or falsity just does not seem to be a relevant consideration for him. He does not care whether, for example, the crime rate in Germany is in fact 'way up' – something he could easily get one of his employees to check if he *did* care. He wants you to believe that the crime rate is up, and so – for that reason alone – he says it. He is, in these contexts at least, simply unmoved by the norm of truth. It's a bit like a child stealing sweets from the shop without even asking themselves the question whether or not they're doing something wrong:

they want the sweets, they have the opportunity to get the sweets, that's all that matters.

We may be wrong in saying that Trump is a bullshitter. Maybe he really believes all of those things. That would make him someone who is attempting to conform to the norm of truth; unfortunately, however, it would also make him delusional. We all know that simply believing things that we would *like* to be true is not a good way to try to conform to the norm of truth. Wanting Serena to win the US Open is not a reason to believe that she will.

We suggest that the concept of bullshit is a useful way of understanding the notion of 'post-truth'. The *Oxford English Dictionary* defines 'post-truth' as 'relating to or denoting circumstances in which the objective facts are less influential in shaping public opinion than appeals to emotion and personal belief'. But the things that tend to get labelled 'post-truth' – Trump's tweets, the output of troll factories, and so on – are, we think, not (or at least often not) appeals to emotion or personal belief; they are instead bullshit. The people making those claims often simply don't care whether what they say is true.

Why does bullshit matter? It matters because telling the truth is important. Our earlier claim that telling the truth is a moral norm was not plucked out of thin air. Things go wrong when people fail to tell the truth. As we saw earlier, if you have false beliefs, things are likely to go wrong for you – you're likely to miss your train, be late for your meeting, or whatever. Trusting people who fail to tell you the truth – believing what they say – is bad for you. Of course, we could – and do – respond to people who fail to tell us the truth by stopping trusting them to do so. That strategy works perfectly well on a local level; no harm done if you don't trust the celebrity gossip columnist or the horoscope writer or that friend who tends to exaggerate their achievements to tell you the truth on the particular topics they're telling you about. But it is bad for us, and for society as a whole, if our trust is undermined on a larger scale. We have collectively learned to ignore the verbal hand grenades of Twitter trolls, but their existence, in large numbers, serves to undermine the trust we place in the testimony of random strangers – a trust we need for all manner of daily transactions. We can only hope that such people confine their bullshit to the internet.

When it comes to politicians, however – and to the news media – lies and bullshit are a really serious problem. If we can't trust *them* to tell us the truth, at least to the best of their ability, we lose our ability to participate effectively in the democratic processes that determine features of our and other people's lives that are much more important than missing a train: student debt, unemployment, a decent health service, climate change, and so on. And if untrustworthy testimony from such sources is allowed to go unchallenged, that might make you start to wonder whether *any* politicians or journalists can be trusted to tell you the truth – and hence to wonder what the point in voting is at all.

We don't, however, have to be merely passive recipients of untrustworthy testimony. Calling people out – holding them to account for their actions – is the way that many moral norms become established and, once established, persist. Think of the #MeToo movement. That's women saying: we have had enough of this behaviour; we're not going to let it pass unchallenged any longer. And that, in turn, is changing the norms that people use to guide their behaviour. Perhaps what we now need is a #TellTheTruth movement. What we hope to have done in this chapter is to help you develop the tools to explain why telling the truth is so very important. We have a lot to lose.

3

Understanding the World

The world can seem mystifying in an enormous number of ways. Quite a lot of questions – like how Wi-Fi works, what the best shape is for a bridge, and how far it is to Betelgeuse – can best be addressed by scientists, but there are plenty of others with which science cannot help us. What is free will? What's the best form of government? How far should we consult relatives' wishes when treating dementia patients? Those are difficult questions and they are all, at least in part, philosophical questions. Other parts of this book have things to say on some questions like these. For now, let us take a step back and consider these two *kinds* of questions and the different roles that philosophy and science can play in helping us to understand the world as a whole.

The right division of intellectual labour is not

always clear-cut; there are questions where cross-disciplinary collaboration is essential. That ought to be no problem: we're all adults, right? Unfortunately it's complicated by the fact that there are a number of scientists with familiar public profiles who think nothing of casually proclaiming that philosophy is dead or useless, or that theology has no subject matter, and other attention-seeking but obviously false things. Their sense of the collaborative multi-disciplinary effort to understand the world is that they are doing all the heavy lifting and the rest of us non-scientists are just spectators, along for the ride or, worse, getting in the way and distracting everyone from science's supposed pure light of objective truth.

So this chapter is about how a proper understanding of what philosophy is and where its boundaries with other disciplines lie can help us to identify and begin to answer distinctively philosophical questions about the nature of the world. In particular we'll look at a few related questions. We will make the case for thinking that there are philosophical questions at the foundations of the scientific project and that therefore there are questions about the nature of the world that are philosophical and not scientific. We will see that science does not have all the answers, and that – really – that's OK. Philosophy doesn't have all the answers either. Science is great;

59

it really is. We have no grudge against science or almost all individual scientists.

One of the questions that a famous few scientists like to busy their leisure time with is the case for atheism. So one way of showing that the remit of science is not as all-embracing as you might think is to show that the question of whether there is a divine or supernatural dimension to the world – a question central to our understanding of the nature of the world and our place in it – is not a straightforwardly scientific (or even theological) question but (at least also) a philosophical one. It is a question that should be sensitive to the input of scientists and theologians, but it's a philosophical question nonetheless. We'll come back to this question below. (Spoiler: we won't be answering it.)

When Richard Dawkins turns on the atheism for a book or an interview, he is dabbling in philosophy if he is doing any more than sounding off. He spends a lot of time despairing of the inability of theologians and religious believers to present evidence of the sort that he would accept – that is, scientific evidence. But if, as we're suggesting, the question at issue is not (or is not only) a scientific one, the demand for only *scientific* evidence is perverse. We're going to examine the nature of evidence in scientific and religious contexts and argue that there is an inescapably philosophical dimension to determining which of our speculations about the nature of the world are justified and which aren't. Let's start with science.

Science makes a whole host of assumptions before it can get going, and these embody philosophical commitments rather than being the results of careful scientific investigation. Take the commitment to scientific experiment itself. It's clear that there can't be an experiment to show that experiments are the way to discover truths. There would be a circularity to trying to prove the value of experiments by doing an experiment, because you would already have to believe in the value of experiments to believe what your experiment told you about the value of experiments! That sort of thing won't do. Our way of proving things has to be independent of the things that we prove using that method. Experiments might be a great way of discovering what happens when you throw chunks of caesium into the bath, but not at all an appropriate way of finding out whether experiments reveal truths.

Thought Experiments

Fortunately there are other ways of finding things out about the world that do not require going out into the field or doing experiments in a laboratory. One tool employed by both philosophers and scientists is the *thought experiment*. In a thought experiment we describe a situation and then we consider what else would happen or what would be true if that situation were really to come about, or we consider whether the situation reveals that we don't understand some important terms that we used to describe it. Thought experiments allow us to consider what would follow from some carefully constructed hypothetical scenario. They won't typically show us what the results would be of bashing *these* particles together with *those*, or starving a fire of oxygen, but they can tell us about some kinds of constraints on the way we're entitled to think about the world. They do this in a variety of ways, but often they start by making us realize what we already think, and then go on to show us that we must be mistaken since what we already think turns out to be nonsensical.

Let's start with a famous thought experiment that allows us to begin to see the point where philosophical and scientific methods meet and could usefully collaborate. Galileo imagined a situation that would test the ancient Greek philosopher Aristotle's idea that heavier objects fall faster than lighter ones. We can paraphrase the thought experiment like this: take an object – a Steinway grand piano, say – and attach it by a piece of string to another object – a poster of Landseer's painting *The Champion*, say. And then without a moment's hesitation drop the whole lot out of an upstairs window. If lighter objects fall more slowly, then the string should soon pull taut as the piano is slowed down by the poster. But the combined weight of the piano, the poster, and the string is greater than the piano alone, so the whole contrivance should fall faster than the piano would by itself. This contradiction – that the combination would fall both faster and slower than a piano on its own – shows that Aristotle's hypothesis must have been false, on the widely accepted grounds that if your hypothesis leads to a contradiction, it can't be true because nothing that actually happens is contradictory. And all of this can be discovered without leaving your armchair or needlessly smashing up any valuable musical instruments. What's doing the work here is not the observational results of practical activity. If we work out that two things would be contradictory, then we know, without doing any other kinds of experiments, that they can't both happen. Going a bit further, we also know that if we try to imagine a situation and we work out that if it happened it would lead to two contradictory results, then we have discovered that we were trying to imagine a situation that is actually impossible. So in this case, Aristotle's hypothesis must be wrong, because if it were right it would lead to two contradictory events – the piano falling both faster and slower than the poster/piano combination.

This illustrates the idea that there are different sorts of evidence we might look for. As well as the kind of physical evidence that tells us all we want to know about how explosions work, or why glasses often smash when dropped, there is the kind of evidence that shows us that two things can't both be true because they would contradict each other. (The sharp-eyed amongst you will immediately say, 'OK, so how do we find out that two things contradicting each other means at least one of them must be false?' Excellent question, but it's one for another book. That book would also be a book about philosophy, or at least about philosophical logic. Anyway, back to this book for now.)

Consider a second example; this time a squarely metaphysical thought experiment. There is a very old puzzle involving a statue. Think of it like this. Imagine that Olive, a sculptor, goes to the river and digs out a lump of clay for her morning's work. Feeling whimsical, she names it 'Lump'. After a cup of coffee and a bit of a think, Olive decides, inspired by the wildlife around her seaside studio, to make a statue of a puffin. This she duly does. By tea-time she has finished, and names the resulting statue 'Puffy'.

Here's the puzzle. It seems right to say that there is now one single physical object on Olive's workbench: Puffy is just the very same thing as Lump. That is a very natural thing to think. But there seem to be some important differences between Lump and Puffy that cast doubt on that thought. One thing we might ask if we want to try to identify an object is, 'When did it come into existence?' In this case, it looks like we want to give different answers for Lump and Puffy: Lump existed earlier, throughout all of Olive's coffee-drinking and thinking time. That suggests that Lump and Puffy are two different physical objects after all.

Another thing we might ask if we are interested in keeping track of an object once it exists is, 'What would it take to make it no longer exist?' Again, it looks as though we want to give different answers for Lump and Puffy. Suppose that Olive decides she can do better and squashes the clay back into a ball ready to sculpt Puffin 2 the next day. It looks as though Lump is still there but Puffy has gone, so again we have reason to think there are two objects on the workbench.

Just as Galileo's thought experiment was an attempt to show that there is something contradictory about the claim that heavier objects fall more quickly than lighter ones, this one tries to show that the claim that there is just one object on Olive's workbench leads us into contradiction: for example, it commits us to thinking that the object both did and did not exist before Olive had finished her coffee. It turns out that our notion of a physical object is not as coherent or straightforward as we thought: there is more work to do. And that isn't something we could have found out by running a practical scientific experiment: no amount of weighing or measuring or finding out more about the chemical make-up of clay, or whatever, would have revealed this problem.

Theoretical Virtues

Another way of figuring out whether one theory is better or worse than another that doesn't appeal to experimental evidence is by measuring your theory against the so-called 'theoretical virtues' like the claim that it is good for your theories to be consistent with each other, or that they should be as simple as they can be whilst still explaining the data. Take, for example, the idea that the earth is flat. You have to do quite a lot of work to make that consistent with the available data, since climbing only a moderately high hill or looking out to sea will give you a strong indication of the curve of the planet, and of course we have photographs of the earth from space now. Sure, you can turn to conspiracy theories at this point and devise any number of obscure explanations for why the government might be out to fool you into thinking the earth is flat, but doing that will make your theory more complicated rather than less. It's much simpler to stick with the explanation that the earth is round; the complexities surrounding the flat earth account don't actually explain any more of the available evidence.

It's not that there is any *scientific evidence* that pushes us towards theoretical virtues like simplicity. Rather they are philosophical claims without which experimental science couldn't carry out its main job, which is gathering data and explaining it to us in the clearest possible way.

We're not trying to catch anyone out here. The fact that science has philosophical foundations shouldn't make anyone feel threatened, or feel as though we're trying to say philosophy can do everything science can do. That would be as bad a misunderstanding of philosophy and its claims as the one that takes it to be dead or useless. The point is just that there's a perfectly good way of understanding philosophy and science that sees them as collaborators in the effort to understand the world as fully as we can.

Evidence and Atheism

We can see the problems that can arise from misunderstanding the nature of evidence by looking at the public discussion of atheism and religious belief. It's a popular field in which it's currently difficult to move for all the scientists. The famous ones have something in common, and that's a firm belief that a commitment to the scientific method and scientific ideals is incompatible with a belief in the existence of God.

Deciding whether there is a supernatural or a divine element in the world is clearly a very important part of understanding what the world is like. The simple fact of believing in God doesn't settle all the questions, of course: it would still be open for discussion whether we should pray, and if so in what ways; what the specific attributes of God might be; whether God has a plan for humanity or not;

and so on. But even without answering those more detailed questions, the plain fact that God existed would make a central difference to our view of the underlying nature of reality. So how should we go about trying to answer perhaps the most obvious of the questions in this area: *does God exist?*

It won't surprise you to learn that we won't be deciding here whether or not God exists. The point of bringing it up is to illustrate one of the ways in which an overconfidence in a certain sort of evidence can potentially lead you astray.

The most vocal of the 'celebrity atheists' of the last few years are scientists. They include prominent physicists and biologists and slightly less prominent chemists. What they have in common for our purposes here is that they think, or they sometimes behave as though they think, that there can be no good evidence in favour of a belief in God. Let's examine that idea a bit.

It's worth conceding straight away that there have been no credible scientifically repeatable instances of people, for example, seeing or chatting with God. You might worry about conceding that at the outset. Does that not decide the matter in favour of atheism? If we give up on this sort of incident as evidence, haven't we pretty much handed victory to the atheist side of the argument?

That should only persuade you to give up the (holy) ghost if you, like the celebrity atheists, think that only one sort of evidence is any good. Atheists should be as reluctant to immediately crown themselves victorious as the religious believers are to concede defeat, because they too should realize that there are other reasons for believing in things than the fact that you've seen them through a telescope or discovered a fossilized one or taken a reading from an appropriate laboratory machine. We've seen that there are more sorts of evidence than the 'causing explosions' kind or the 'glasses smashing when dropped' kind. We should at least see whether those other sorts of evidence have anything to contribute in this area as well.

And, of course, they do. How? Well, for example, it could be like this: if we take seriously the idea that science can't answer all the kinds of questions we might be interested in, then we can imagine a possible theory that gives us a reason to believe in God on the basis that it includes God as the simplest systematic way of explaining all the evidence. We said above that explaining the available data in as economical a way as possible is a theoretical virtue. That fact in itself is compatible with the claim that God exists, or the claim that the earth is flat, or the claim that the Queen is a lizard. If it turns out that there are observations that can be explained most economically by a theory that takes any of those claims to be true, then we have at least some reason to believe those claims. As with all our theories, if the overall body of evidence changes – if we make new observations or we discover one of our existing beliefs to be false, for instance – then we should change our minds. In our view, at the moment the data and observations we have available suggest that the simplest theory of how the world is doesn't include any of these claims.

But if we devised or happened upon a systematic theory of the nature of the world that included God, if the theory was good at explaining the world to us and it included God as an essential part, then that would, on the face of it, give us theoretical evidence for the existence of God. If an explanatorily useful theory says that God exists, and also that electrons exist, and both things are essential for the theory to successfully explain things for us, then it might seem obvious to think that there must really be both electrons and God.

We'll come back to God in a moment, but first let's explore a little more the idea that if a theory is the simplest explanation of the things we observe, like footprints in the butter, then the things it talks about, like fridge elephants, must really exist.

Understanding the World

Evidence and Explanation

Do the results delivered by science reveal to us (at least part of) the way the world really is? Well, our current best scientific theories include reference to electrons, and these theories are very successful at explaining a huge variety of things, from the most complex chemical reactions to the reason the light comes on when we flip the switch. Some philosophers think that the success of our theories gives us good reason to believe that the world contains electrons. Other philosophers argue that we should say, perhaps more cautiously, that the success of these theories shows us only that the systematic way of talking that includes talk of electrons is good at helping us predict what we'll see next time we switch on the oscilloscope. This second group of philosophers say that what we get from scientific experiments is a systematic way of understanding the world that brings with it no commitment to thinking that there is a fundamental reality that matches the description delivered by physics.

At first glance that might look like an odd thing to think. What could it mean to say that science doesn't discover the way the world really is? Isn't that the whole point of science? The world is the subject of its experiments, isn't it? Don't microscopes render visible some of the things that are otherwise too small to see? It could start to seem like those stereotypes of philosophers wondering whether their chairs really exist might have been on the money after all.

It may also be true that most – or even all – scientists turn out to agree with the first group of philosophers. Still, that wouldn't show there's no question here to answer, only that most scientists have picked an answer and are not interested in having that debate. And that's fine: the debate won't make any difference to how successfully they do their work. It just isn't something you can tell by doing more science, and doing science is their thing.

If you buy the idea that there's a philosophical debate to be had here, you might be wondering how we can go about settling it. As always, we need to consider the evidence.

In many cases in our ordinary lives we need a kind of evidence that is broadly similar to the sorts of evidence delivered to us by scientific experiment, and we will go about collecting it in roughly the same way. If we want to know whether it's true that the quickest way to get to the swimming baths is to go straight across Sandhurst Square and cut through the park opposite Whitehaven Mansions, then we'll time ourselves going by that route, time ourselves going by some likely-looking alternative routes, and compare the results. If we want to know whether it's true that Grub-Gone cleans your towels better than New Improved Washo, then we get some of each and try them out. But in some cases the sense in which we 'gather evidence' can be rather different.

We've seen that we can do thought experiments to discover that two hypotheses are contradictory and that therefore both can't be true together. There's nothing that is in general esoteric or unfamiliar about this other sort of evidence gathering. Consider the investigation of a crime. There will, of course, be aspects of the inquiry that call for empirical, even straightforwardly scientific, evidence. Does this swab taken from the whisky glass at the crime scene contain the DNA of the chief suspect? On the other hand there will be the kinds of questions that call for an investigator to look for a way to systematically embrace all the empirical evidence at once and come up with an explanation of the crime as a whole.

Think of the way that Hercule Poirot disdains the frantic physical effort of less subtle detectives. 'Oh, Hastings, Hastings. Always for you the dashing about! You must learn to employ your little grey cells! Mark my words, *mon ami*, the solution to this mystery is to be found in the psychology of the criminal; it would have been quite impossible for a man of the type of the Colonel Bollington, with the habits most orderly, suddenly to fly to Paris, take up a poker, and dash out the brains of the nephew of his wife merely for the sake of a few hundred pounds!'

This is not just a statement of empirical evidence. The realization that sets Poirot apart from Hastings is that to tie the loose threads of the case together what's needed is not just another piece of evidence of the same kind, but a piece of evidence at a more general level that can tell us something about how all the other pieces of evidence must fit together.

Something similar is going on in the debate we've just described about whether our best scientific theories reveal the way the world really is. What we're looking for is some implication of taking a side in that debate that will conflict with something we are very sure is true. For example, scientists are often able to make successful predictions based on their theories that assert the existence of electrons, or dark matter, or what have you. Some philosophers think that this success would be utterly mysterious if those things didn't really exist, and that this sort of mystery is best avoided if at all possible.

Even if in the end we can find evidence to help us

decide between philosophical positions like these, why does it matter if it makes no practical difference to science itself? Well, it's important to get the fullest account we can of how the world works and what the world in its most general terms is like. Science is a part of that but not the only part, and not, as it turns out, the most general part.

Think of it like this. If you bake a cake, you need to make choices about your ingredients. You choose your sugar, your fat, your flour, and so on. You know that the information you're gathering to help you make your decision doesn't call on you to consider the world in its most general or abstract terms; you're very much focused on the immediate practical matter of getting the cake to rise properly. You're well aware, as you do all of that, that there is more to be said about sugar than whether it gives you pleasant treacly notes, or whether it blends easily with water to make smooth icing, but right now you don't care. Other people care, and the world is richer for their caring; you wouldn't want them not to care, but you're interested in more immediate questions like the richness of this particular buttercream. Let those other people worry about how carbon bonds to hydrogen and whether there are eleven or twelve oxygen atoms in a molecule of sucrose; you know it's important in principle, but so is cake and you can't do everything at once. It would be a distraction to most of us to worry too much about molecular structure while we were trying to beat air into a Victoria sponge.

In our more scientific moods we wonder about precisely those things. And we find them fascinating. We know that baking is interesting in itself, but right now we just want to quickly eat this slice of cake so we're not too hungry to get on with taking readings from this hadron collider we've built.

Of course, baking, on the one hand, and physics and chemistry, on the other, aren't the only ways in which we might be interested in the world. Just as the scientist might look at baking and think that it doesn't examine the world in a sufficiently general way for her liking, so the same happens in the other direction. A shopkeeper selling cakes is likely to care little, when she has her commercial hat on, for the intricacies of baking, and less still for the atomic weight of hydrogen. She knows those are fine and worthwhile things to be interested in, but they're irrelevant to the problem at hand, and there are other people better qualified to take care of that sort of thing.

And so, without any great leaps, or any rejection of the usefulness of science, or any suggestion that philosophers know better than scientists how to approach distinctively scientific questions, we might look at science and think that, fascinating and worthwhile though it is in its own terms, and useful as it is in contributing to a full understanding of the world, still it doesn't examine the world in a sufficiently general way for *our* liking. Don't worry, scientists: baking doesn't do that either, and baking is more important than either science or philosophy! But still, we know that baking powder will make a cake rise but that won't tell us, no matter how often we make delicious, light, fluffy cakes, what it is in general for one thing to make another thing happen. And going in the other direction, answering the question of whether the relation of a cause to its effect is just a matter of regular patterns of things of one sort succeeding things of another sort wouldn't help at all if what we were trying to do was build a power station: we'd only want to know how to get some sort of fuel to cause enough force to drive a turbine and produce electricity.

Shopkeepers aren't in competition with bakers. Bakers don't imagine that scientists are trying to tell them they don't know how to make caramel. All of that would be ridiculous: evidence of misunderstanding at best, paranoia at worst. Scientists do not need to think that philosophers are trying to muscle in, or that we are claiming to know better than they do how to do science. Metaphysics just asks questions of a more general and abstract nature than physics. Both sorts of questions are interesting, legitimate, and worthwhile; both sorts of questions contribute to the greater project of trying to understand the world as fully as we can. To succeed in that we need scientists and we need philosophers. And we certainly need cake. And also biscuits.

Only once we make certain philosophical assumptions can we engage in other modes of inquiry. If we assume that the world is a world made up fundamentally of objects – roughly, bits of material *stuff* – then it makes sense to start doing empirical investigations of the sort that science is great at. If we don't start from that assumption, but assume that there are both physical and non-physical aspects to the world, or we refrain from making any such assumption in advance, then it's open to us, for example, to devise theories of the nature of the world that include God.

To take an example: there are those people who believe we need religion as a basis for morality since science cannot by itself answer questions of value. That view may be held without any inconsistency even by people who think that science beats religion when it comes to explaining evolution and rejecting creationism.

We don't take the view that religion is required as a basis for morality, but we also don't think that all views of this sort can be rejected in advance. Theories like that must be considered in an open competition with other theories that don't include God, otherwise we'd just be begging the question: that is, assuming part of what we're supposed to be trying to prove. Testing one version of a religious worldview against another is a different question from testing religious worldviews in general against non-religious worldviews in general. We should start our investigations without any assumptions that second-guess the answer we might get, otherwise the way we consider the results of the investigations will be tainted by those assumptions and our comparisons are less likely to be fair ones. Our biases will play a role in determining which results we get, and that will make the results useless for persuading other people that we have got it right.

We should also keep in mind that whatever the upshot of the atheism debate – God or no gods, religion or atheism – deciding which theory we should eventually prefer to all the others would again be a matter that called for philosophical input. Which theory is simpler? Are all the competing theories consistent within themselves and also consistent with other beliefs that we're reluctant to give up on or revise? These are inescapably philosophical questions.

It's unlikely that all religious believers would be happy with the result that the best theory was one that included talk of God, but also said that this didn't imply that God *really* exists, because our theories can only ever hope to be useful ways to systematically organize and consider our experiences and not guides to any underlying reality. But if that turned out to be where the evidence, taken in its broadest sense, points, then that's what we should believe.

'What's the message that we should take away from all this? It can't all just be about cake, can it? At *most* life is only 40 per cent about cake.' Well, you're forgetting about the biscuits, but you're basically right. The most important thing for our purposes is to notice that if our goal is to understand the world, understand all its aspects in ways appropriate to every level of detail and abstraction, then we need philosophy just as much as we need science. And, in order to understand in specific detail all the other areas of our cultural and political lives, we also need history, economics, theology, and so on. These disciplines are not, or shouldn't be, in distracting conflict; they should be in productive collaboration. That's at least part of why philosophy matters to understanding the world.

4

Understanding How to Behave

Unless you've been raised in complete isolation as part of some misguided social experiment, one of the guiding factors of your life will have been and will continue to be your interactions with other people. Every time you have a meal with a member of your family, speak on the phone to a friend, pay the shopkeeper for your shopping, ask a passer-by for directions, go to your doctor to have a rash looked at, play the Apollo Theatre with your grindcore band, or give out free ice cream on Fifth Avenue dressed as a bee, you're interacting with people. Perhaps less obviously, tagging someone in a tweet, or complaining about someone in a book, also constitutes interacting with them.

And those interactions are, in many obvious and also in many subtle ways, policed. Sometimes that policing is literal. We may quite rightly be arrested for pushing someone into a hedge and stealing their hat. Sometimes the policing is more internalized and relies on our knowledge of social and ethical norms that are supposed to govern the actions of well-behaved citizens. There are guidelines that we all know that constrain the sorts of things you're allowed to shout at a person in the street; there isn't an exhaustive list of impermissible shouts, but we have a good idea of where the line is that we must not cross, though we may not all draw it in quite the same place. Moreover, we seem to start developing a moral sense quite early on, though of course at first it is often focused on trivial things and can be quite self-centred. As children we might be passionately concerned with questions of right and wrong in the form of resenting the unfair distribution of sweets (fair enough: nobody wants to get less than their fair share of sweets) or demanding the right to stay up later now that you are nine years old, like your brother is allowed to.

Morality and the Law

The boundary between the two sorts of policing is porous: there are certainly things that you might shout at someone in the street that could see you arrested by the real live police. We're not going to put ideas in your head by telling you what some of them are. If you're not sure where the line is, aim to stay well on this side of it. On this specific example, your rule of thumb really ought to be: 'Don't shout anything at anyone in the street unless it's essential as a way to warn them of an oncoming tram.' On the other hand, sometimes the law allows a variety of possible verdicts in a given case, and the courts have to indulge in some ethical reflection to decide which of the available penalties would be the right one to give out. In this way philosophy is central to another aspect of our public lives.

Ethics is that branch of philosophy dealing with, to put it very simply, right and wrong. It has been central to the discipline of philosophy since its beginnings and through all of the various traditions across the world. As with the other branches of philosophy we've discussed so far, a lot of the subject matter of ethical reflection is very familiar. We have all faced decisions with ethical dimensions: decisions about our personal behaviour, our political preferences, healthcare, or whatever.

The interactions we began with are ones in which everyone is routinely involved in the course of a perfectly ordinary life, but there are other sorts of interactions as well, for example those that are forced on you in light of your professional obligations. Just think of some of the cases we have seen already and consider them from the other side: there are carefully written rules about how a doctor is allowed to treat her patients and how a police officer must respect a person being taken into custody. Of course, in these more formally regulated kinds of case, just like our more mundane ones, there are also numerous unwritten but widely accepted moral codes. The moral codes and the law might also meet in the middle in the form of some sort of charter of professional best practice. In an ideal world these codes, laws, and charters will have been drawn up with the help of some philosophically informed reflection, perhaps even with the help of professional philosophers.

On a broader scale there are the rules that govern the way the society considered as a whole, or the government as the embodiment or representative of that society, is allowed to treat its citizens and the citizens of other countries, whether those people are within its borders or elsewhere in the world. On the international stage we have rules about when it is legitimate to go to war, knowing that many people will die. Closer to home we have, for example, the obligation on the government to guarantee that every child has access to free education.

We can talk in a general way about 'rules', but of course these rules include both formal laws and moral norms or codes. To see the difference between moral requirements and legal requirements, consider the selling of guns in supermarkets. There is no question that there are jurisdictions in which, at the time of writing, this is legal. But there is a serious question over whether it is moral. Waiting until your friend leaves the room and then eating all her biscuits is also immoral – a very low-down trick indeed – but we'd hazard a guess that nobody thinks it should be a matter for the courts.

Things can also be illegal without being immoral. For example, think of a law against homosexual sex – a matter of (uncomfortably recent) history in the UK and the USA, but still in force in other jurisdictions around the world – which makes illegal something against which there is no cogent moral objection to be made.

Two other things might strike you immediately about the examples of rules governing sex and education. First, they are rules that have changed over time; second, they are rules that not everyone across the world agrees on. There is, for example, disagreement over minimum legal school leaving ages. Some people have seen that as evidence that whether something is right or wrong depends in part on where and when you find yourself and what the people around you think. The strongest form of this idea is called 'moral relativism'. The basic thought is that moral decisions and judgements are true only relative to a particular locally current code. What's tempting about this is precisely that this is how a lot of moral decisions *seem* to be made. Naturally when we want to decide whether something is good or bad we start from the general ideas that our own society has, and that we've grown up and become familiar with, of what makes things good or bad.

However, it is important to remind ourselves that we make a lot of moral decisions quickly, based on the received wisdom about what general sorts of things are right and wrong – and even some quite specific instances of actions that we have been told are right or wrong – and that the received wisdom itself might not be morally defensible. Examples of actions that were once sanctioned by law and approved by large numbers of people but which were morally indefensible probably leap readily to your mind. Many of the worst involve the systematic suppression or persecution of minority groups – or, in the case of the oppression of women, majority groups who have been systematically deprived of the social and political power to assert the strength of superior numbers – and that is not something that you ought to accept, no matter how many people disagree with you. That's not to say that it would be easy to stand up against this if everyone disagreed with you, of course. That would be to trivialize the incredible struggles that have been endured even to get us to today's imperfect position. Challenging these injustices, these immoral laws and unjust social norms, is worthwhile – more than worthwhile, it's necessary – but it is hard.

Think about the political issue you find most important, or that you're most passionate about. The way you arrived at your view on that issue was probably not by doing a head count to discover how many people you would be agreeing with. Instead you wondered whether your view was supported in the right kind of way by good arguments. One of the main benefits of philosophical thinking is that it enables us to find, or at any rate to look for, the right kind of justification for our actions – that is, a justification that appeals to critical thinking and rational reflection rather than to emotive rhetoric or majority voting. More than that: it *forces* us to try to give this kind of justification. Anything less than a good reason of this sort will just not do. So in the case of moral relativism, we need to be able to determine whether the prevailing moral view is justifiable or not, and we don't resolve that question by settling for the answer that it must be right because it's what most people round here think.

Morality and Religion

If we are dismissing the idea of moral relativism, what is to go in its place? One historically popular option is to subordinate all the various moral codes to a single religiously inspired code. That immediately gives you the universality you wanted, but any given religious code of ethics comes only if you also commit to some metaphysical claims about the nature and absolute authority of God that many people will explicitly reject. Moreover, there is a famous problem for the idea that we should refer to the word of God to find out what is good and bad. It is based on an idea explored by the ancient Greek philosopher Plato in a dialogue called *Euthyphro* (pronounce that something like 'youth-i-fro', with a short 'i' like in the word 'it'). Plato's concern is piety and he talks of *the gods* rather than of God, but we can adapt the example without losing the essential point.

The so-called 'Euthyphro dilemma' is this: does God approve of good actions because they are good, or are good actions good because God approves of them? A dilemma is a situation in which there are two possible conclusions: you have to go for one of them, you can't have both, and neither one is desirable. Each of the options is called a 'horn' of the dilemma, and the situation forces you onto one horn or the other. Let's start with the first horn of the Euthyphro dilemma: the claim that God approves of good actions because they're good. If that claim is true, then there must be an independent standard of good against which actions must be measured, even by God – so the standard of good and bad is not God after all but something to which even God has to look for answers.

What about the second horn: the claim that an action is good because God approves of it? If *that* claim is true, then it leaves it open that if God decided that setting fire to giraffes for fun is the high point of morality, then the high point of morality recreational giraffe incineration would be. But it's surely absurd to suggest that morality is hostage to God's whim in this way – and it *would* be a whim, because, according to this horn of the dilemma, God is not constrained by any independent moral standard. Of course there are plenty of ways in which you might respond to Plato, but if you want to disagree with him then it's your responsibility to say why his argument fails. However, it is at least worth seeing whether we can find a basis for morality that doesn't rely on God.

There are, as you might expect, plenty of options on the table when it comes to finding a non-religious basis for morality. Our purpose here is not to come to a conclusion about which moral theory is right. That is something it's certainly worth thinking about for yourself, whether as part of a broader systematic engagement with philosophy or not. What we are keen to do is impress upon you the importance of taking time to assess your existing opinions and taking steps to make sure you have good reasons for believing the things you believe. Examples of things taken as central by philosophers in judging the moral quality of actions include human rights, wellbeing, motive, equality, character, and happiness. Every one of these gives us a potential basis for our moral judgements that does not appeal to a divine lawgiver.

The various approaches deliver the same verdict in a wide range of cases. Respecting human rights often also produces the greatest level of wellbeing in the general population. This common agreement is what you might expect, since there are plenty of things we all agree are wrong or permissible or morally required. Before any of us learns any philosophy there is likely to be pretty widespread agreement amongst a wide variety of people that, for example, stealing someone's wedding ring is wrong. Whatever formal moral code we end up adopting, even if we adopt it only for the time being and accept that we might need to work to revise and improve it, we want it to have as one of its results that stealing someone's wedding ring, or setting fire to their giraffe for fun, is wrong. If the different moral theories are doing their job properly, they will tend to agree on the uncontroversial cases.

Making Moral Decisions

Our moral lives are messy. Often there seems to be no obvious best course of action and we are left to choose between several unpalatable options. In those sorts of cases we can appeal to theories that have a good track record of explaining the rights and wrongs of our behaviour to help us to see what might be the rights and wrongs of the messy cases. The widely agreed cases can to a certain extent act as a way of calibrating our moral theory: if it gets the result that burglary is fine, maybe it needs a tweak. Not that you should unhesitatingly commit yourself to whatever judgement you think a particular theory would make, of course. The idea always is to consider the results of your application of your theories and not turn them into dogma. Reflect, reflect, reflect.

Let's look at a familiar example. Suppose you are motivated to be vegan on the basis that it is indefensible to cause the suffering of animals by farming them for meat – or for other food like milk, eggs, or gelatine, or for other products like leather. The idea that something should be avoided or prevented because it causes suffering is a philosophical idea. The most famous version of this sort of idea, utilitarianism, argues that the morally right action is the one which, on balance, causes the best ratio of pleasure to pain: we should act in whichever way is most likely to produce the most pleasure and the least pain.

In practice this is extremely difficult to predict accurately, but it's relatively easy, at least in pretty normal cases, to predict roughly. We may not know exactly how much animal pleasure would be caused by stopping farming animals for food or exactly how much animal pain would prevented, but we can make educated guesses based on some empirical investigation and some already generally accepted thoughts. That is, the difficulties are things like not knowing enough about the relevant species' experience of pain and pleasure, not knowing how many animals there would be in subsequent generations if numbers were not being kept artificially high for commercial exploitation, and so on. These questions are important for the utilitarian because the amount of pleasure will depend both on the nature and intensity of the pleasure or pain and on the number of things feeling pleasure or pain at that intensity or in that way.

Of course, you don't have to take this sort of philosophical position in order to be motivated to be a vegan. Other moral theories are available! To take just one more, you might be motivated to avoid using animal products on the grounds that to do so would be evidence of a regrettable aspect of your own character, perhaps that it would reveal you to be arrogant or exploitative or discriminatory, and that where possible you want to correct character flaws of this sort. Someone taking this sort of line would be an advocate of *virtue ethics*, which says, roughly, that our aim is to work out how to be the best kind of person we can be, to develop the best kind of character we can, to be virtuous instead of vicious, in order that we might, individually and collectively, live the best lives we can.

It's also not true to say that any of these general moral theories guarantees you any particular conclusion on broad personal or social questions like eating animal products. There's nothing intrinsic to virtue ethics that means you automatically end up being a vegan. The same goes for a moral theory that has its basis in judgements about what your duties are, what rights and responsibilities you have, how much happiness there is in the world overall, and so on. In each case more theoretical work, and often also empirical data, are required before we can reach a definite conclusion on a clearly stated specific moral question.

Some judgements that we might make in our contemporary context about what is right or wrong might really not have been right or wrong in other circumstances. For example, suppose it is right to guarantee people who don't have the use of their legs access to a wheelchair. That seems clearly to be the morally right thing to strive for. But in a situation in which wheelchairs would be useless – in a location with only rough tracks rather than smoothly surfaced roads and footpaths, for example – the obligation to provide them would disappear. What this illustrates is that the thing that made the action of giving someone access to a wheelchair morally right was never something intrinsic to a wheelchair. Rather it was about the important right of everyone to some measure of freedom and autonomy and the obligation on us all to provide that for each other. What was really motivating the obligation we currently have to provide access to wheelchairs for those who need them was a more general obligation to provide everyone with means to move around where they like, have access to public buildings and spaces, and so on. The specific obligations are generated by the interaction of this deeper obligation with the specific local conditions: if those local conditions include rough tracks that make wheelchairs useless, we would incur other specific obligations in order to meet the deeper obligation.

Or consider an example an old friend of ours used to use to illustrate the difficulty of deciding a course of action based on a desire for equality. Suppose you have been commissioned to provide public toilets and have been asked to take into account the need for equality between men and women. That might seem easy, until you start to draw up the plans. Do you aim for equality of expenditure, giving you more facilities for men than women on the grounds that urinals are cheaper than cubicles? Do you aim for equality of queueing time? Equality of capacity of the facility at any given moment? Each of these will need a different distribution of your resources and will require you to build a different set of structures. This simple example neatly illustrates the interaction of theoretical considerations with real-world practicalities. We can't do all of our thinking in splendid isolation from the real world where the difficult problems are, otherwise we'd miss the input from other disciplines and the empirical evidence that should guide our decision making. On the other hand, we can't do all of our decision making without rational reflection, otherwise we run the risk of latching on to the first solution that comes to mind and missing the subtleties that will only appear after careful thought. If you take only one thing away from reading this book, it wouldn't be a disaster if it was this: things are always more complex than they seem.

You might worry that these examples commit us to just the moral relativism we earlier rejected. In the wheelchair case we said that whether it's right to provide people with wheelchairs varies with context. However, our reason for saying that was that there is a general principle concerning equality of access that applies across *all* contexts. After all, the claim wasn't that in situations where surfaces are too rough to make wheelchair use possible, no obligations are incurred; only that some *other* way would have to be found of ensuring equality of access. A moral relativist, by contrast, will claim that this general principle itself – the right to equal access – is one that holds in some societies or cultures but not in others.

The Value of Moral Philosophy

Moral philosophy won't give us the answers ready-formed, but without it we are in a significantly worse position to work out how to behave. Here, as elsewhere, philosophy is a tool that we employ in order to help us think clearly about difficult questions. Thinking about the most important moral questions in this sort of careful way helps us to make sure we're disagreeing about the right things. Ethical discussions can become passionately heated because they involve the questions about which we feel most strongly. Imagine being as intensely interested in the outcome of an obscure debate between civil servants about whether a new form should be called '807/E' or '807/D(2)' as you are in the outcome of a debate over whether people should be given the mobility assistance payments that the form is used to apply for. If we don't take considerable care to remind ourselves that it would be fruitless, it's easy to get angry at people who disagree with you about fundamentally important things like political equality or military intervention.

We all know from our own experience that in fact getting angry about this sort of thing doesn't change anyone's mind. It might even have the opposite effect, causing people to dig their heels in and refuse to listen to your arguments. Of course, they might do that anyway, but there's certainly nothing to be gained by goading them into it. Much better to at least begin with the assumption that people who disagree with you are not just simpletons or beasts and that they are capable of understanding reasonable arguments if you take the trouble to formulate and present them. This sort of approach forces people who disagree with you to explain exactly why it is that they have a different view. You can, for example, explain to them why their proposed social policy will have the effect of reducing access to help for the people who need it most and how that is likely to result in increasing distress and misery for many, which you take to be a bad thing because you are committed to equality of opportunity and economic disadvantage is the biggest single driver of disenfranchisement. That way they are forced to give you an argument either as to why the policy will not have that effect or as to why that effect is not problematic in the way you think. Then you will know whether to concentrate your efforts on persuading them that it will have that effect after all or on persuading them that economic inequality is actually bad or maybe, if they already see all of that, on persuading them that they should be interested in avoiding bad things happening even if they're not happening directly to them.

These sorts of exchange can be infuriating – there's no doubt about that – but if we conduct them whilst infuriated they will certainly be fruitless. We're not saying that philosophy has a magic way of making you less infuriated; in many situations it can make you more infuriated by helping you to see either the nature and scale of the problem or the likely difficulty involved in addressing it. What it can do at its best is to allow us to consider the sorts of general principles at work in complex situations. We might be able to come to see a particular disagreement as a confusion about which moral duty is really being ignored, or a failure on the part of one side to resolve a contradiction at the root of their position. As we've said, philosophy is a tool – or rather a set of theoretical tools – that can help you to engage in a fruitful way with real moral problems so that, with a bit of luck, we might come closer to being able to resolve them.

Understanding how to treat each other, what our obligations are, what we are permitted to do or forbidden from doing – in short, how to behave

Understanding How to Behave

– is fundamental to our social lives and the questions are, at least in part, distinctively philosophical ones.

Conclusion

Now you've made it through to (nearly) the end of this book, you are – we very much hope – in a position to think more seriously about why philosophy matters. But before we get back to that important question, we want to talk briefly about areas of philosophy that we haven't covered. We've talked about questions concerning who we are, whether we ever act freely, the nature and proper use of evidence, the differences between philosophy, science, and religion, how we ought to behave, and so on. But there is a lot more to philosophy than those particular questions.

Take art, for example. You might have found yourself in a gallery looking at a work of contemporary art – a pile of tyres, say, or some artfully (or not) arranged bits of rusty metal – and asked yourself the old chestnut, 'Yes, but is it art?' And you might have followed that up with '… and if so, why?' Before modern art came along, philosophers tended to think that art was all about beauty – but there's (arguably) no beauty in a pile of tyres. Does the mere fact that the pile of tyres is being displayed in an art gallery suffice to make it art? Must the person who made the artwork (or arranged the ingredients) have intended it to count as a work of art? These are all philosophical questions, of course – to be answered not by conducting experiments or opinion polls but by thinking: by (for example) carefully considering what does and does not count as art, and then trying to figure out what distinguishes what does count from what doesn't. This might perhaps involve constructing thought experiments. (If I took the pile of tyres and carefully arranged them in the same way down at the rubbish dump, would they still constitute a work of art, or would they just be a pile of tyres? What if the tyres had somehow found their way into the gallery by accident, and the staff had left them there assuming that they were a new exhibit?)

Or take politics. Why – if at all – is democracy better than dictatorship? After all, in principle a benign dictator might turn out to be a lot better at delivering a fairer, more equal, more prosperous society than the democratically elected government of a society whose population contained sufficiently many mean-spirited and selfish people to have elected a government that cared not at all for things like fairness, equality, and prosperity. Is a representative democracy – where government policy is based on the votes of members of parliament who (supposedly) represent the interests of their constituents – better or worse than a direct democracy, where the population vote directly on policy rather than voting to elect other people to decide those matters for them? Is the first-past-the-post system of voting that determines which candidates get elected to parliament in the UK fairer or less fair than various forms of proportional representation, where the proportion of MPs who are members of a given party closely matches the proportion of people who voted for that party? Should a government aim solely to pursue the interests of its own citizens, or should it aim to contribute to making the world a better place for people elsewhere as well – for example by providing aid – at the expense of its own citizens?

Or take death. Is it rational to fear death, given that while you are alive death hasn't happened to you so it is not harming you, but once you are dead you will not be in a position to be harmed by it? Or – going to the other end of life – at what point after conception does a fetus acquire a right to life that outweighs the pregnant woman's right to choose what happens to her own body?

What about disability: does disability constitute an intrinsic harm or deficit in a disabled person, or is it instead a construction of the society we live in? (Imagine a built environment made for giants so that none of us could use the stairs. Wouldn't we all be disabled in such an environment? There's another thought experiment for you.)

We could go on – at great length. There is barely an aspect of human life or an area of inquiry that doesn't throw up interesting philosophical questions. There are philosophical questions to be asked about morality, religion, and politics; about race and gender; about physics, chemistry, and biology; about the language we use to describe the world or to vent our feelings or to try to persuade someone to let us have the last slice of cake; about ... well, anything at all, really.

And we haven't even talked about other philosophical traditions. The sort of philosophy we work on, the tradition we identify with most strongly, is what is known as 'analytic' philosophy, named for the logical and subsequently linguistic analysis of its twentieth-century originators. 'Analytic philosophy' is increasingly unhappy and restrictive as a name for a field more diverse than this historical echo suggests, and it's not really a name that has made it into the popular consciousness, so it would be unhelpful to use it, but if you see it anywhere, that's pretty much what this book has been doing.

This sort of philosophy can reasonably usefully be distinguished from the tradition more prevalent in France and other places in continental Europe, which as a result is sometimes called 'continental philosophy'. That tradition shares a very large number of ancestors – and indeed much of its subject matter – with the sort of philosophy we work on, but it has seen a lot more influence from literary theory, psychoanalysis, and radical politics. And then there is Indian philosophy, Chinese philosophy, African philosophy, Islamic philosophy, African-American philosophy, Hispanic philosophy ... the list goes on. You can't read very much into the various names on their own: Indian philosophy, for example, is no more *about* Indians than continental philosophy is about Swedes, Poles, and Belgians. By contrast, African-American philosophy *is*, to at least a great extent, about philosophical issues arising from the historical, political, and cultural context within which African-Americans live. There are all kinds of interesting commonalities of – and differences between – subject matter, methods, and more general approaches to philosophical questions that run between and within these areas of philosophy.

Having persuaded you, we hope, that philosophy really is everywhere, let's get back to our original purpose: to persuade you that philosophy matters. We said in the introduction that philosophy matters because it seeks and promotes understanding and clear thought, and because it is practically helpful, intrinsically interesting, and culturally and historically significant. Let's examine those claims, starting with the first one.

One thing we hope to have done in the course of this book is, precisely, to promote your understanding of, and help you think clearly about, a range of philosophical issues. You might, for example, have started out wondering whether all those neuroscientists are right to say that there's no such thing as free will, but not had the least idea how to go about investigating that question. Now, we hope, you have at least got some sense of how you might make some moves in that direction. (There is, of course, a lot more to be said on that topic!) And in making those moves you will, inevitably, be required to think clearly and carefully. You will need to ask yourself what, exactly, the argument is supposed to be that takes us from the neuro-scientific data to the claim that free will does not exist, and you will need to ask yourself whether it is a good argument: are its assumptions true? Does the conclusion follow from the assumptions? And to answer those questions, you will need to think about the various concepts involved: what is it to be in control of your behaviour? Can you be in control of what you do even if you could not have behaved any differently? And what does it mean to say that you could not have behaved any differently in the first place? As you progress you will, precisely, be understanding the issue better and thinking more clearly about it. And this will be so even if – as is often the case – you end up still not being sure what the answer is to the question you started with. Understanding isn't simply a matter of knowing the answer to a given question. You might know – on the basis of the testimony from mathematicians, who are very reliable on such matters – that every even number is the sum of two primes, and yet not have any understanding at all about why this is so. Going in the other direction, a mathematician might spend their entire career trying to prove a conjecture that nobody has ever managed to prove before, and fail. They have failed to answer the question they wanted to answer, but they will have come to understand a lot more about the maths than they did at the outset. Doing philosophy is often – perhaps almost always – a bit like that.

Next: we claimed that philosophy is culturally and historically significant. We'll make just two points to justify that claim. The first concerns science. The distinction between philosophy and science is, in the grand scheme of things, a relatively recent one. Back in the seventeenth century, when Isaac Newton was busy getting bonked on the head by an apple and inventing the concept of gravity, what he took himself to be doing was 'natural philosophy' – that is, roughly speaking, philosophy as it applies to the natural world, rather than as it applies to religion or ethics or whatever – like his predecessors. Newton's great work, *Philosophiae Naturalis Principia Mathematica* (*Mathematical Principles of Natural Philosophy*, 1687), was intended to be in dialogue with René Descartes's *Principia Philosophiae* (*Principles of Philosophy*, 1644). Today we think of Descartes as a philosopher and Newton as a scientist, but back then most of the experimental techniques that deliver the kind of empirical evidence that is used to justify or adjudicate between different scientific theories hadn't been invented yet; actual empirical evidence, at least in many of the domains that we now think of as the sciences, was pretty scarce. So 'natural philosophers', to a great extent, proceeded much as philosophers do today: by thinking about stuff and coming up with theories; and even their experimental work was often founded on assumptions that we would today regard as distinctly unscientific. (Newton was an alchemist as well as what we would now think of as a physicist.)

Going back further into the past we see a similar pattern. Many of the ancient Greek philosophers were not just philosophers but physicians, anatomists, pharmacologists, and cosmologists as well. In the second century AD, Galen of Pergamon even wrote a treatise called *That the Best Physician is Also a Philosopher*. And in the extraordinarily rich intellectual environment that was the Islamic world in the Middle Ages, again the great intellectuals were often all of the above, as well as religious scholars. It's something of an irony that in universities today 'interdisciplinary' studies are often regarded as a rather newfangled invention, whereas in fact the very idea of distinct autonomous 'disciplines' is itself relatively recent. And – importantly for our purposes – as far back as human beings have been thinking in a systematic way about the world around them, philosophy has been at the very heart of it.

Our point here is that – to put it bluntly –

historically speaking, it's entirely likely that without philosophy, there would have been no science. It was the philosopher's quest to understand the world that led to the development of the kinds of experimental technology and techniques that now constitute the backbone of scientific method and practice.

The remaining two claims we made in the introduction were that philosophy is practically helpful and that it is intrinsically interesting. How – apart from promoting clarity of thought and careful attention to evidence and argument, which are unquestionably useful in most walks of life – can philosophy be of practical use? Well, frankly, quite a lot of it *isn't* of any practical use; many issues that some philosophers devote a lot of time, and sometimes entire careers, to investigating have no practical consequences at all. Nothing in everyday life really hangs on whether, whenever you have two things – a chocolate cake and a nice cup of tea, for example – you automatically have a third thing, namely a chocolate-cake-and-nice-cup-of-tea. ('Of course you don't!', you might say. But you probably believe in crowds, which are just collections of people, and houses, which are just bricks and mortar appropriately assembled. Why believe in crowds but not the chocolate-cake-and-cup-of-tea?)

Come to think of it, nothing in everyday life really hangs on whether you think there are any good reasons to believe that the world outside you exists at all, rather than being just a highly sophisticated computer simulation. As a matter of psychological necessity you're going to carry on believing in the external world, no matter how strongly you feel the pull of a philosophical argument to the effect that you have no good reason to believe in it. Try it if you don't believe us. (Of course if you were ever to find yourself breaking out of the simulation one day, as Neo does in *The Matrix*, then things would certainly be rather different.)

It's important not to over-generalize to *all* of philosophy, however. For one thing, you can never be quite sure which arcane-seeming bit of philosophy might turn out to become crucial to something really rather practically important. Alan Turing, widely regarded as one of the fathers of modern computing, basically invented the field of artificial intelligence by asking the distinctly philosophical-sounding question, 'Can machines think?' So you can blame him when the robots take over and enslave us all. But, more importantly, plenty of philosophy *is* practically useful – at least in the sense that plenty of questions that we ask ourselves for the purposes of making a decision about how to act are, at least partly, philosophical ones. Is it permissible to lie to my friend when he asks me if I like his new haircut? Is it OK to vote in the election given that I really don't have a good grip on the issues involved and would just be going on gut feeling? Can I legitimately be rude about that really ugly bit of contemporary art, or should I consider the possibility that its purpose is something other than looking pretty?

Moreover, plenty of philosophers are directly concerned with practical questions: is marriage a good or a bad thing? Is it morally acceptable to eat meat? In what circumstances is genuine consent given – to sex, say, or to a medical procedure? What kinds of weapons should be subject to international bans? Is pornography a form of hate speech, and should it therefore be made illegal? And so on, and on.

Of course, as we've seen consistently throughout this book, being able to think clearly and in a well-informed way about the question doesn't, unfortunately, necessarily yield an answer you can be hugely confident about – which, when it comes to practical action, admittedly makes philosophy rather less useful than you might want it to be. But think of it this way: if you have equipped yourself with the resources to think clearly and in a well-informed way about the question, at least you can be pretty confident that – however you then go on to behave, whether it's going vegan (or not) or telling your friend that his haircut is dreadful – you are not behaving that way out of sheer ill-informed muddle-headedness. And we're taking it as a given that acting out of sheer ill-informed muddle-headedness is not a good idea. If nothing else, you will at least be able to justify your actions – to yourself or to anyone who tries to take you to task. Your friend may not be that impressed that you told him the truth about his haircut thanks to being convinced that Kant was right that the imperative to tell the truth is a universal moral law, but at least he can't accuse you of being thoughtless.

On the second claim – that philosophy is intrinsically interesting – all we can really say is that we find it so, and so have countless other people throughout history and throughout the world. We hope that you have found this book intrinsically interesting as well. If you haven't, well, philosophy isn't to everyone's tastes. (And even if it is in principle to your taste, this particular book might not be. Go ahead and try another one; you might like it better.) But we'd be very surprised if you managed to go very long without accidentally stumbling across a philosophical question. We hope that when that happens you will at least now recognize it as such. Perhaps you'll even find yourself wanting to figure out how you might go about answering it.

Further Reading

General

There are very many introductory philosophy books out there; you can easily find recommendations on the internet. For a taster on continental philosophy – something we didn't cover at all in this book – you might try Simon Critchley's *Continental Philosophy: A Very Short Introduction* (Oxford University Press, 2001).

By way of giving even more of a sense of the diversity of topics and traditions that philosophy encompasses, you might like to visit the following two major philosophy podcast sites. *History of Philosophy Without Any Gaps* (https://historyofphilosophy.net) is a vast and growing resource of podcasts covering – amongst other things – classical, Islamic, medieval, Indian, and Africana philosophy. *Philosophy Bites* (http://www.philosophybites. com) contains hundreds of interviews with philosophers on a huge range of topics – from bioethics to Buddhism, feminism to friendship, sustainability to sports. Use the

Further Reading

search box to look for podcasts on many of the topics discussed or mentioned in this book.

Chapter 1

The first part of the chapter dealt with the topic of personal identity; try David Shoemaker's *Personal Identity and Ethics: A Brief Introduction* (Broadview Press, 2009). If you found the discussion about the psychological and brain differences between men and women interesting, you might like this online lecture by Cordelia Fine (a psychologist): http://www.abc.net.au/radionational/programs/philosopherszone/the-galaxy-of-gender/6563092. For free will, try Helen Beebee's *Free Will: An Introduction* (Palgrave Macmillan, 2013).

Chapter 2

For a general theoretical introduction to epistemology you could try Jennifer Nagel's *Knowledge: A Very Short Introduction* (Oxford University Press, 2014). If your interests are more practical, Harry Frankfurt's *On Bullshit* (Princeton University Press, 2005) explores the topic of bullshit in much more detail, and has the virtue of being only sixty-seven pages long; you could also listen to Miranda Fricker's *Philosophy Bites* podcast on 'epistemic injustice' (http://philosophybites.com/2007/06/miranda_fricker.html).

Further Reading

Chapter 3

For an overview of the philosophical discussion of science, you could have a look at Samir Okasha's *Philosophy of Science: A Very Short Introduction* (Oxford University Press, 2016). There's a nice blog on the relationship between science and the philosophy of science by Janet D. Stemwedel on the *Scientific American* website (https://blogs.scientificamerican.com/doing-good-science/what-is-philosophy-of-science-and-should-scientists-care/).

Chapter 4

Philosophy Bites has lots of episodes that apply philosophical thinking to moral questions; you might try Rebecca Roache on the rights and wrongs of abortion (http://podcasts.ox.ac.uk/rights-and-wrongs-abortion) or Julia Annas on virtue ethics (http://philosophybites.com/2014/12/julia-annas-on-what-is-virtue-ethics-for.html). There is a nice section on atheist ethics in Julian Baggini's *Atheism: A Very Short Introduction* (Oxford University Press, 2003), which also covers some of the other ideas introduced in chapters 3 and 4.